HOW TO SPEAK WITHOUT FEAR

SMALL TALK COURSE:

YOUR STEP-BY-STEP GUIDE TO MORE COMFORTABLE, CONFIDENT, AND COMPETENT SMALL TALK

IN ALMOST ANY SOCIAL SITUATION

Signe A. Dayhoff, PhD

How to Speak Without Fear Small Talk Course: Your Step-By-Step Guide to More Comfortable, Confident, and Competent Small Talk in Almost Any Social Situation

Published by Effectiveness-Plus Publications LLC
80 Paseo de San Antonio
Placitas, New Mexico 87043

Cover by Signe A. Dayhoff and around86 @ fiverr.com

ISBN: 978-0-9985324-1-7 (Print Ed.)

Welcome!

You're here because you want to conquer your fear of small talk and get the benefits that small talk provides.

- Perhaps you'd like to make friends more easily.
- Perhaps you'd like to socialize or date more comfortably, or
- Perhaps you'd like to network and make job connections more effectively.

As you're about to discover, you can do all that ... and a lot more ... in *only* 10 Modules!

I'm Dr. Signe A. Dayhoff, your Social Effectiveness Coach, at Effectivenessplus.com. As a Social Psychologist, I have put together this course based upon my personal experience with fear of speaking and small talk, my research in social anxiety and interpersonal skills, but mostly based upon what you have told me you really want in order to be more comfortable talking with others ... whether in informal or formal situations ... in your personal and work lives.

The motto of this course is that: *Whatever you want could be only one casual conversation away.*

TABLE OF CONTENTS

Building Your Success Foundation

Before we get started on building your success foundation, I have a little exercise for you to do along with me. I want you to put your right hand straight out in front of you and move it in a circle clockwise.

Okay, now, at the same time you're doing the clockwise circle with your right hand, I want you to make a figure six with your right foot. What happens?

Everything seems to get all uncoordinated. If you're thinking it's because you can't walk and chew gum at the same time, that's not the problem.

Think of your hand as being your *desire to make small talk* and your foot as being your *fear about making small talk*. Your fear can dictate the degree to which you can achieve your desires.

Now … I want you to move your right hand again in a clockwise circle, but this time when you add your right foot, begin the figure six from the *inside* of the figure and work your way out. What happens?

That's easier, isn't it? Instead of your hand pushing and your foot pulling, your hand and foot are going in the same direction— both pushing. What this demonstrates is that when you control your fear of small talk, your desire to make small talk can work unfettered. Together they provide a sort of synergy to enable you to achieve your goal. In this course you will be creating that synergy.

As you'll soon see, this course is jam-packed with tips, suggestions, examples, techniques, and laser-focused exercises. This is *everything* you need to increase your social confidence, competence, and effectiveness ... to reduce your fear of speaking, and master conversational skills ... to accomplish your small talk goals.

As a result of alleviating your self-presentation fear and confidently handling small talk, you will find that you can literally be *only one casual conversation* away from getting whatever you're seeking. Let me illustrate this:

David was in Barnes and Noble, browsing through the mystery section, looking for paperbacks by Tony Hillerman. Another person approached the shelves as David was searching and pulled out a book. David could see it was *Coyote Waits* by Hillerman.

"Oh," said David to the stranger, "I was looking for that one too. I've really enjoyed the PBS Mystery productions of Hillerman's work so I'm looking forward to reading them all."

"Do you like to write?" asked the stranger.

"Well, yes, how did you know?"

"Just a guess. If you'd be interested in learning how Hillerman does it, he's offering a course next month at Santa Fe College."

"No, really? Hey, that's great. Thanks for letting me know." David grabbed a copy of Hillerman's *The Thief of Time*, all the while thinking about finding a place to sit so he could open his laptop to locate the course announcement and sign up for the upcoming course before all the seats were gone.

BEFORE YOU START

How do you become a more confident conversationalist? The bare bones answer has five components:

- *First* you have to know specifically what you want to achieve.

- *Second* you have to develop a step-by-step plan to achieve it.

- *Third* you have to create the small-talk success mindset.

- *Fourth* you have to learn the essential small-talk success strategies.

- *Fifth* you have to practice, practice, practice and act, act, act to do it with patience and persistence!

I'll bet you're saying to yourself, "Yeah, you make it sound so simple, BUT ...." Yes, I know. Hard as it may be to believe, mastering small talk *isn't* some big, complex process or deep, dark secret.

Becoming a confident conversationalist is a lot more straightforward than you probably think. In fact, it's based upon your simply acting on a spelled out set of principles, guidelines, and general rules ... in a graduated, systematic fashion, following them step-by-step.

Overall, all you really need to do is to learn how to till, fertilize, and water your conversational soil so your small-talk seeds will take root naturally, grow, and blossom.

For example, David, whom you already met, wasn't always so eager to talk to strangers. In fact, he dreaded it because he had no idea what he would say or how it would be received. Before he worked on his small-talk skills, he never talked to strangers, unless it was an emergency. Instead, he kept his eyes averted so he wouldn't make eye contact and then have to do something. Just the thought of having to open his mouth with a stranger turned his hands clammy and stomach into knots. His brain ceased to work.

Okay, you may be thinking, if it so easy, why has it seemed so difficult in the past?

It's not because you didn't know what the problem was. No, that was pretty obvious to you. And ... it wasn't because you didn't have the motivation or you didn't make the effort to do it. No, if you're like most people struggling with fear of speaking and small talk, you tried and tried ... until you threw your hands in the air in frustration.

What was the cause? The cause was that you didn't *yet* know that there were things you needed to know in order to do it. After all, how many of you ever had someone take you aside to explain what you needed to discover? Darned few, I'll bet! And how many of you were ever taught formally how to meet people, make conversations in this situation or that, and then build on them? Even fewer, I'll bet.

It's also because you didn't have the help of someone well-versed in the subject to guide you every step along the way. Someone to help you lay your groundwork, set your course, and help you avoid the pitfalls. You didn't have the coach you needed to keep you focused and on target until you reached your goal.

That is, until ... now!

Over these 10 modules I will mentor you to achieve small-talk mastery by providing you with everything you need: Conversation principles, strategies, tips, examples, scripts, and exercises galore. *But* the most important component of this course is what you will discover and develop as a result ... the "Speak Without Fear Small Talk" mindset.

The "Speak Without Fear" mindset is so powerful that it will replace your currently unproductive mindset with a success-orientation. It will make all those principles, strategies, tips, examples, scripts, and exercises stick like glue ... once and for all.

You can say "good-bye" to negative, ineffective habits. You can say "good-bye" to conversation anxiety and feelings of inadequacy. Instead, you can say "hello" to the small-talk competence and confidence you have dreamed of.

I break each step in this comprehensive and field-proven small- talk program into small achievable tasks for you work on and accomplish. With each task you'll test your developing capabilities. With each task completion you'll build your confidence, competence, and effectiveness. Each completed task will be another brick in the foundation of your small-talk mastery.

Research has shown that success leads to increased self-confidence ... and self-confidence, in turn, leads to success. This is a positive feedback loop. It reinforces itself. Everything this course employs is reinforcing. Therefore, everything you do as part of this course will support and enhance everything else.

However, even though the course is 10 modules, that doesn't mean you have to do it in 10 weeks. When I was personally coaching people through this course, it might potentially take only 10 weeks but that was 10 hard, intense weeks with me constantly guiding them.

You, however, should take you time and do it at your own pace BUT do it *regularly*. Make it a continuing process: Once you've finished one chapter, its assignments, practiced the principles and examples, and truly feel you understand it, then—and only then— should you go on to the next chapter. This isn't a race. It's a learning experience so you have to tailor the course to your learning style and timing.

PREPARATION FOR GETTING STARTED

Before we get started, there are three things you need to do in preparation. This is the essence of your Pre-Module 1 Assignment. Before you actually launch into the Module 1, there are certain essential things that you *must* do:

You need to start a daily record of what you're doing for this course and what results you are getting.

You are to assess your current small-talk skills' level. For example,

- How do you feel (emotionally and physically) when you think about making small talk? *(Note in space below)*

- What thoughts run through your head? *(Note below)*

- How do you respond? *(Note below)*

- With whom can you speak? In what situations? *(Note below)*

You need to do this in order to gauge your progress. You have to know where you started in order to see the changes for the positive that have occurred.

You are also to determine your small-talk goals. For example,

- Do you really want to speak confidently in social situations? If so, why? *(Note below)*

- Do you really want to make friends more easily? If so, why? *(Note below)*

- Do you really want to network or socialize at gatherings? If so, why? *(Note below)*

This Pre-Module 1 Preparation Assignment is so important ... so foundational ... that I want to go over it with you now in detail to make sure you fully understand for what it is asking.

But first, you need to create your *Speak Without Fear Daily Journal.* You may find an 8 ½" x 11" loose leaf notebook is the most versatile for all the writing you will do. I've allotted space in the book for you to take notes. These notes should then be transcribed into your Journal. In your Journal you will record all you do in this course. This includes everything from this Preparatory Assignment on.

Now I'm going to have you write down what there is about making conversation *specifically* that bothers you. And don't say, "Everything," even though that may be how it feels right now. I want you to *spell out* the specific behaviors that are the problem for you. For example,

✓ Does approaching someone of interest seem threatening?

✓ Is finding something to say after "Hello" the difficulty?

- Okay, so what specifically bothers you about speaking to strangers and others and making small talk? *(Note below)*

If you have any information about how your discomfort with small talk may have come about, provide it. For example,

✓ Were you ever humiliated by an adult, sibling, or school mate when you tried to make small talk?

- What happened to make you feel uncomfortable speaking to strangers and others and making small talk? *(Note below)*

Next, you are to detail your concrete and specific goals for your small-talk mastery. This to be in terms of positive behaviors – what you *want to be able to do* – and *NOT* what you don't want to do. For example,

✓ "I want to feel confident speaking to others" - NOT "I don't want to be anxious speaking to others."

✓ "I want to be prepared with things to say" – NOT "I don't want to stand there, looking at my feet because my mind's gone blank."

These will likely mirror what you said bothered you about small talk.

As you become aware of your daily experiences with small talk (both positive and negative), you are to record them *briefly* in your Journal. I emphasize "briefly" because I don't want your journaling to feel like you're writing a term paper.

To help focus what you write, you are to use the following questions to describe each experience. I'm going to list the questions first. Then after I do, I'll give you examples of them:

- What happened

- Where and when it happened

- What your thoughts were Before, During, and Afterward

- What your feelings were Before, During, and Afterward

- How your body felt Before, During, and After the experience

- What your behaviors were Before, During, and After.

Instead of writing a full account with lots of detail, you are to *simplify* and *crystallize* the experience as much as possible. That is, get rid of extraneous material and keep doing and redoing it until you can get to the core of the experience.

To do this use *keywords in sentence fragments*. This does take a little practice because we all tend to ramble and feel each element of the event is important.

Let me give you examples of what you're going to write:

- ✓ What happened – *Boss wanted to talk with me and I panicked*
- ✓ Where and when it happened – *Noon in front of my office*
- ✓ What your *thoughts* were Before, During, and After the experience –*(Before) "What have I done wrong," (During) "I can't think of anything to say," (After) "I just babbled; the boss is going to think I'm an idiot."*
- ✓ What your *feelings* were Before, During, and After the experience – *(B) fear, (D) frustration, (A) disgust with myself.*
- ✓ How your *body felt* Before, During, and After the experience – *Heart racing, shallow breathing, sweating, blushing (B), (D), (A).*
- ✓ What your *behaviors* were Before, During, and After the experience – *(B) I looked at my feet, put my hands in my pockets, (D) started to speak, but nodded instead, and (A) hid in my office.*

Keep This in Mind: This awareness takes time to cultivate. It's likely you haven't had to be aware of all this before or in such detail. As a result, you should not expect to ace it the first, second, or third time you do it. You didn't learn to tie your shoelaces the first time you tried that either.

Believe me, *nobody* does this quickly or "just right" at first. So do your best with it. Keep plugging away at it … and suddenly you'll have an "aha!" and you'll have it. It *will* come. "You CAN master each incremental step toward making successful small talk!"

As the course will demonstrate, it is simply a matter of

- Changing your thinking about it—that it's an opportunity, not a threat
- Knowing what to do—being prepared with strategies, tips, scripts, and templates
- Knowing how to do it—getting each step of the step-by-step process under your belt
- Knowing when and where to do it—initially locating your specific audience, later being able to generalize to any audience
- Employing practice, persistence, and patience— acting on it until it becomes a habit for you.

Reminder: Your goal is to absorb and assimilate everything in this course. The objective is not to simply do each assignment but to work on and with each of them until you feel you have incorporated the thoughts, feelings, and behaviors into your own behavioral repertoire. You want it to become a part of you. That is, you need them to become a *new functional habit* that replaces the *old dysfunctional habit.*

Furthermore, for each Assignment I've left you space to write or make notes. I recommend that you answer any questions on each assignment page and then transfer it to your course Journal. Any thoughts about the exercises and assignment as you go through should also be committed to your Journal. PLEASE don't skip creating a course Journal for yourself. Because it employs using other senses as well, it can reinforce your thoughts and feelings. It also allows you to see your own progress. These things can make all the difference in how you enjoy the course and how well you do in it.

Module 1

Let's Start by Looking at Small Talk

WHAT IS "SMALL TALK"?

In common parlance, small talk is any superficial personal communication between two or more people. It's the vehicle through which you and others approach each other to test to see if there is any interest in getting to know one another, pursuing topics or interests.

Conversation can be achieved in a number of ways. It can be through automated communication, such as e-mail, iPhones, cell phones, texts, social media, blogs, and voice mail as well as in person. However, it's the in-person talk that's not only the most anxiety provoking but also the most *effective* and *productive* in achieving your relationship goals with anyone in any situation, from personal to work. Consequently, when we talk about Small Talk here, we are referring to in-person, face-to-face communication.

WHY IS IT IMPORTANT?

While it's called "small" talk, there is definitely nothing "small"—or trivial—about it.

Conversation is important because it's essential to establishing rapport. And rapport—mutual trust or emotional affinity—is *the* basis of *every*—not just most—

but EVERY relationship. This means that every relationship *begins* with it and *depends upon* it to keep it going.

And … as you already know … relationships are important because they are the foundation of *everything* that really matters to us as humans, from personal to work life.

The point to remember is that it's virtually impossible to meet and get to know people—to feel a sense of trust and closeness and to form relationships—without simple, casual conversation. It doesn't matter what the situation is: Whether it's meeting with a job interviewer or speaking to someone of interest at a social gathering. Face-to-face talking matters!

WHY IS THAT SO?

Let's look briefly at why this is. Communication that is automated, like texting which uses shorthand is less personal and effective because there is a greater degree of anonymity and ambiguity. You have less real information with which to work and the information isn't always clear or straightforward. Consequently, there's a high potential for misinterpretation and misunderstanding.

Moreover, with having minimal nonverbal input (like eye contact, facial, hand, or body gestures, intonation and inflection, for example) automated communication lacks the texture, depth, emotion, sensitivity, and richness of face-to-face communication. As cell phone cameras are employed more in conversations, this may change to some degree. But these pictures will still provide less of what it takes to create significant relationships. This may be because we're a bit more conscious of being filmed and the impression we're making which is being recorded and could become permanent.

Small talk is what makes the first connection and lets you get the ball rolling as you become accustomed to the other person's style, voice and speech patterns, mood, and energy level. It smoothes the transition from nothing to whatever it is you want to talk about. And it disguises any awkward moments that you may feel as you settle into discovering the other person.

In-person small talk possesses the qualities necessary for forming our most meaningful relationships ... from friendships to intimate relationships to work and business relationships.

IS SMALL TALK INNATE OR A LEARNED SKILL?

If you're like most people, you will tend to believe that the majority of people have no problems with meeting and conversing with strangers. They just manage somehow. However, surveys have repeatedly shown that up to 95 percent of the U.S. population reports that it was truly *un*comfortable talking with strangers. And this was especially true when the strangers were in a group. Moreover, with the popular advent of cell phones, people have tended to become more insular and anonymous, unconsciously relying on their phones rather than on in-person social interaction when they had a choice.

In spite of this, and while it may seem otherwise, small talk skills are NOT innate. They are *learned* and *developed*. They can be learned in many ways. For example, you learn them by using confident people as models and imitating their small talk behaviors. You learn most of your social interaction vicariously early on from your parents or guardians.

Another way is simply trying one thing after another to see what works for you. This tends to happen later on in your development. This trial-and-error process is how most of our much later learning occurs. Even when you watch others and mimic their behaviors, you are still testing to see what works for you, as well as what doesn't. This means you have to find what is comfortable for your personality and preferences.

WHY DO SO MANY FEEL UNCOMFORTABLE WITH STRANGERS?

There are six reasons for this:

First reason is that certain negative core beliefs were hammered into your head as a child. You know the ones, like: "Don't talk to strangers," "Don't speak unless spoken to," "Don't be pushy," "Be humble—don't toot your own horn," "Better to be safe than sorry," "Good things come to those who wait."

David, for example, heard most of these as a child but really resonated to, "Be humble and don't toot your own horn." As a result, he felt that talking about himself was a tacky and immodest thing to do that would show others that he didn't know the "social rules." He was sure he'd be negatively evaluated if he spoke up.

These admonitions, and others, have made you wary and reluctant to interact with those you do not know ... or don't know well. They have made face-to-face interaction seem like a risky proposition.

Second reason is that because so much of your

communication today is automated and anonymous, your everyday in-person communication skills can become "rusty." In some instances, it may even seem as though you didn't have these social skills in the first place. Consequently, you can feel inadequate in social situations with new people ... and even with people you know.

For example, Dinah was sure that she hadn't a clue about how to talk with people. Her father had told her repeatedly, "Children should be seen and not heard," so as she grew older, she tried less frequently to engage others.

When you don't know what to expect and are unprepared for interactions, you will tend to find ways to trivialize the necessity of small talk. You will tend to discount and dismiss its usefulness. And when you demean it, you can then feel justified in rejecting it and trying to avoid this kind of interaction.

Dinah, in her mind, would laugh at how boring small talk was. Consequently, she had no desire to listen to nonsense about garden club activities or who had a new Lexus or scored the winning point in high school basketball.

Third reason is that with all of the above factors comes an elevated level of shyness in our society. It seems to be related to a generalized feeling of isolation, alienation, and low-level social anxiety. This is something many people in Western cultures increasingly feel today.

Fourth reason is that for those for whom generalized social anxiety—or even stage fright—is a more *significant* problem there is the *additional* fear of negative evaluation, being found inadequate, and rejected. This can make face-to-face meeting and small talk be something to be shunned.

As you probably know, fear of speaking in front of others is America's #1 fear. This fear pertains not only to giving speeches but also to making conversation, networking, being interviewed, promoting yourself, and making presentations. Fear of speaking publicly is so strong that it leaves fear of death well behind. Now, that is saying quite a bit about its significance.

Comedian Jerry Seinfeld once quipped that at a funeral most people would rather be in the casket than giving the eulogy. The same goes for speaking with strangers.

Fifth reason is that you tend to believe there is *one* and *only one* way to accomplish small talk. That is, there is a right way and a wrong way—that there are strict black-and-white rules that you *have* to follow ... and follow *perfectly*—or not at all. In other words, you may believe that if you don't know how to execute small talk correctly and perfectly, you are guaranteed to fail ... and will be a social flop.

Both David and Dinah believed perfectionism was essential so as to rule out the possibility of someone finding something wrong with their small talk. But as they could never quite reach so-called "perfection," they opted instead to keep their mouths shut. The problem with trying to be some conception of "perfection" is that you cannot control how others will choose to evaluate you. It's purely subjective. They can think whatever they think irrespective of what you do.

Sixth, and final, reason is that you tend to believe that successfully making small talk is the result of special knowledge that only certain people have. Those people have it because they were born with it. And, *if they were born with it, there's no way YOU can get hold of it.* The result of this belief is that you will (1) believe it's smarter and safer not to try and (2) not try.

Module 2

What Do You Need to Do to Prepare to Speak Without Fear?

Before we look at any of the strategies, guidelines, and rules of making small talk, you will need to work on three (3) foundational areas. These are the building blocks for your small talk skills. They are absolutely essential to changing your negative patterns into positive ones. In fact, without them you are likely to continue to spin your small-talk wheels, leaving you immobilized.

These foundation stones are:

- Your thoughts and beliefs
- Your physiological arousal
- Your behavior.

We'll work on each of these separately.

THOUGHTS AND BELIEFS

These are your automatic negative thoughts and negative self-talk about speaking to people that constantly swirl in your head. They are also the maladaptive core beliefs (like "Don't speak unless spoken to") on which they are based.

Many of this come from *forbiddances* you learned in

childhood that later morphed in *allegiances* and *loyalties* to those who expressed them. For example, my mother was artistic but her father-in-law severely criticized her efforts to everyone. Demoralized, she stopped showing her paintings. Unconsciously, I felt an allegiance to my mother in this area. To show my illustrations and paintings would be disloyal to her especially if they did well. So, for years I didn't express my artistic desires either and sabotaged my potential success. I didn't want her to feel bad.

These automatic thoughts and erroneous beliefs work together. When you don't believe you can or should do something, like talk to others, you will say negative things to yourself to justify avoiding doing so, as Dinah did.

PHYSIOLOGICAL AROUSAL

When you think fearful thoughts, your body goes into overdrive. Your heart races. Your breathing becomes rapid and shallow. Your brain seemingly disconnects from your tongue. You can go blank and can't think of a thing to say. While you're in this panic mode, relaxation is impossible ... *unless* you have the right coping tools and strategies to reduce your anxiety.

Thus, to be able to think and act effectively you need to shift your focus from inside yourself to outside yourself. But being focused requires your preventing, interrupting, or countering these fear thoughts. And, preventing, interrupting, and countering these fear thoughts requires your taking control of your physiological arousal.

BEHAVIOR – When you do not know how to make small talk, you are unsure of what to say and what to do. You don't know how and when to use verbal and nonverbal behavior. You feel you don't know the "rules of the road" so you avoid face-to-face meetings. Avoidance means you physically escape or desperately want to. The problem with escape is that when you avoid the feared situation, you don't test the reality of your fears to see if things really are as you expect them to be. Moreover, when you escape, you reinforce "escaping" as the way to deal with the situation which only embeds it more deeply.

We'll be working on automatic negative thoughts, maladaptive (erroneous) beliefs, dysfunctional physiological arousal, and avoidance behavior over the next several modules.

DEEP-SIXING SABOTAGING THOUGHTS AND BELIEFS

The first foundational stone with which we'll work is the automatic negative thoughts and beliefs that have kept you from being ready to work successfully on your small talk.

Your beliefs about talking to people (for example, "Don't talk to strangers," "Don't speak unless spoken to," "Be humble—don't toot your own horn," Don't be pushy," "Better to be safe than sorry," "Good things come to those who wait" and "Children are to be seen and not heard," for example) set the framework for your automatic negative thoughts about conversation. This means that before you can look at your thoughts about small talk, you need to discover your underlying negative core beliefs ... and examine them closely in order to eliminate them.

Assignment

Your first assignment is to look at your negative core beliefs. Before you can change your negative core beliefs to positive ones, you have to know what they are. You need to begin by cataloguing these beliefs as specifically and concretely as possible.

- Think back to when you were a child and you were receiving all sorts of messages from adults, other authority figures, and the culture about speaking up. Most of them were warnings or strict standards for your behavior. What were they? *(Note below)*

- After you recall them above, write down as many as you can think of in your *Speak Without Fear Daily Journal.*

By the way, don't be surprised if these core beliefs come back to you slowly ... at first. After all, they're in your sub-conscious. Moreover, these aren't something you tend to consciously think about very often. But as you do start to remember, you will tend to remember them more easily. They may include some I have already mentioned.

WHAT DO YOU DO ABOUT NEGATIVE CORE BELIEFS ABOUT SMALL TALK?

Once you have your list of negative core beliefs, you will need to begin to challenge the truth or validity of each of them. Even if you have only a short list at first, you can start to work on it. You need to challenge them by asking what concrete proof you have that these beliefs are really.

It is important that you note as many examples as you can think of where they are NOT true. This is because it is harder to accept something as true when you have lots of evidence to the contrary. You will use a similar disputation method to attack and eliminate your automatic negative thoughts.

As I said, your negative core beliefs are the basis of your automatic negative self-talk. Your automatic negative self-talk is made up of thoughts about small talk that you just can't seem to get out of your head. You know the ones. They're there all the time ... buzzing around ... defining your reality.

Negative self-talk consists of statements like, "I've always had trouble meeting people," "It's just the way I am," "I can't make small talk," "Who wants to make small talk anyway," "It's boring," "No one wants to hear what I have to say," or "They'll think I'm stupid." Do any of these sound familiar?

Assignment

You will now begin to address your automatic negative thoughts that are based on your core beliefs.

- Write down as many of your negative core-belief-based <u>thoughts</u> as you can. For example, if one of your negative core beliefs is "You shouldn't talk to strangers," a negative thought growing from that belief would be, "I should avoid talking to all strangers." *(Note below)*

- Write down what inferences comes from each of your automatic negative thoughts about small talk. For example, one inference from the negative thought "You shouldn't talk to strangers" is that "Strangers are dangerous." *(Note below)*

- Now, take each negative thought and turn it around into a positive statement. For example, for "Strangers are dangerous" you would make it "Strangers can be ____ (helpful, interesting, etc.)." It's important to note that when you turn the negative thoughts around into positive thoughts, you should NOT use the word "not," as in "Strangers are *not* dangerous." "Not being dangerous" is not the same or as positive as "Being safe." This is the beginning of your changing your current small talk mindset. *(Note below)*

* * *

In order for you to increase your awareness of your automatic negative thoughts, you need to track them and record them nightly in your *Speak Without Fear Daily Journal.* The more aware you are of them, the more readily you can dispute them and eliminate them. You may be surprised how often they pop into your mind ... just under the radar. So as often as you can, make note of them. It is difficult to remember them at first, especially since you haven't thought of them as negative, but they will become easier to remember as you work on it.

DISCOVERING YOUR VULTURE

Another way to think about your automatic negative thoughts is that they represent a Vulture sitting on your left shoulder, constantly whispering fear-thoughts in your ear. The Vulture sees you and everything around you through a selective, negative filter. As a result, the Vulture has nothing good to say. The Vulture is what you currently believe and how you think about yourself, outside events, and whether you should try anything new "if you could possibly succeed."

However, on your right shoulder sits your Coach. The

Coach sees everything realistically, objectively, and more positively. The Coach doesn't use a selective filter. Instead, it deals with things as they come, as they are, and assesses them analytically. The Coach looks for what can be positively derived from the situation and learned to make things better next time. One can always learn something positive from a situation, even a bad one.

Your Coach is the one who will address and dispute the Vulture's irrationality. It will do so by countering what the Vulture says with facts, concrete and specific evidence, and reality. Initially your Coach is very small because the Vulture has had all the negative-thought-and-belief power control over you. This means that your Coach will have to dispute the Vulture's automatic negative thoughts vigorously and frequently from the beginning.

As your Coach out-reasons and out-evidence-supports the Vulture, your Coach gets bigger and stronger. As you become more adept at disputing your Vulture, your Vulture will shrink. And finally, it will disappear, leaving you feeling positive and confident.

SLAYING YOUR VULTURE

As you become more and more aware of your automatic negative thoughts, you will focus more and more on disputing them. *Remember.* The thoughts and inferences the Vulture makes are inaccurate, emotionally biased, and irrational. Your Coach needs to address each objectively, rationally, concretely, and specifically.

- YOU START BY SAYING: *"That's not true because..."*
- ✓ For example, if your Vulture says, "Your report was a flop because you couldn't remember the latest figures," your Coach gathers one piece of concrete evidence to discount what the Vulture says and supports a more positive and realistic interpretation, "My boss did say my research was helpful to her decision making about the proposal."
- Actually saying "That's not true because ..." helps put the situation into perspective—why it is not as dire as you initially felt and believed it to be.

- NEXT YOU SAY: *"A more accurate way of seeing it is ...."*
- ✓ For example, "It was really only a small omission in the overall comprehensive report." When you can see it more accurately and objectively, looking at the whole from a distance, it will also lessen your catastrophizing about some specific and generalizing it to the whole, like saying, "The boss is sure to fire me for doing this."

- WHEN CATASTROPHIZING THOUGHTS APPEAR, YOU SAY: *"The more likely outcome of this is ...."*
- ✓ For example, "The boss will ask me to give her the latest figures and have them available for my next report." This forces your mind to disengage from the feelings of anxiety or panic and look more logically at the situation, the context, implications, and likely consequences.

- WHEN YOU ARE CONFRONTED WITH SOMETHING THAT DIDN'T WORK OUT AS YOU HAD INTENDED OR WANTED, YOU SAY, *"One thing I can do about it ... now or in the future ... is ...."*
- ✓ For example, "I could have a check list of all documents I need for the report and check off each document 30 minutes before the meeting as I put them in my folder." Rather than feeling really bad about making a mistake (and beating yourself over the head about it), step back from it and see how you can use it as an opportunity to learn and do better the next time.

Remember: Mistakes are what make success possible! You can't be successful without them.

* * *

Important: To makes these statements even more believable and acceptable to your mind, it is imperative that you explore your experience to find examples of them. This is because you must anchor each positive statement in either a direct or indirect positive related concrete, specific experience. In other words, make it something you experienced personally or something you saw happening to someone else. Without this evidence-anchoring, your mind will discount and dismiss it as nonsense ... as feeble attempts to fool yourself into believing what it "knows" is not true.

Assignment

- Go back to your negative core beliefs and provide examples from your experience that illustrate a more realistic and positive interpretation. *(Note below)*

- Begin recording what your Vulture says to you. Pick one Vulture statement each evening to dispute. Go through the Coach's process to show why what the Vulture says is emotionally biased, irrational, and not anchored in reality. *(Note below)*

- The greater the number of evidentiary anchors you have, the greater your Coach's power and the more you will be willing to believe what your Coach says. Record everything in your *Speak Without Fear Daily Journal.*

* * *

Note: All that these exercises require is that you think seriously about them and take your time doing them. It is better to take a little more time up front to locate, dissect, and dispute your maladaptive core beliefs and their related automatic negative thoughts, than to hurry on to the next exercise. You are not competing to finish this course with anyone, even yourself.

Your objective is to transform yourself into being free to speak to others. You can think about this process any way you like, as a form of meditation or even free associations. It's whatever mindset works for you to get you into the zone to do the work.

Never forget that these negative beliefs and erroneous thoughts are toxic baggage you have been lugging around with you for decades. They have been negatively influencing all you do and how you do it. They have controlled you by making your afraid.

You need to get rid of them or they will continue to poison you, your attempts at small talk, and will further erode your self-confidence. Your overall comfort and conversational success depend upon it. We'll talk more about Self-Talk shortly.

Reminder: Keep disputing your anxiety-related beliefs and thoughts as they pop up in your mind.

- Carry a small notebook with you so you can jot them down as they occur.
- The small-talk anxiety Vulture is constantly whispering failure statements in your ear.
- As long as you don't dispute them, you are accepting them as gospel.
- Your feelings and actions will reflect those poisonous whispers.
- Your Vulture will be and stay in control of your life.

If, however, you listen to your Coach and follow its advice, you can counteract the Vulture. This is because the Coach is encouraging to you to analyze everything the Vulture says, to demand hard evidence, and accept reality over irrational negative emotion. The more you do this the more self-assurance, comfort, and competence you gain through the Coach.

Recognize that your thoughts and expectations, whatever they may be, create your emotions and behaviors. Note also that each can influence the other and be influenced by it as part of a feedback loop. If you expect failure, you will think and feel like a failure. If you think and feel like a failure, you very likely be a failure on the task at hand because you will unconsciously find ways to obstruct yourself.

Don't forget:
- What and how you think affects what and how you feel.
- What and how you feel affects what and how you do.
- When you feel negative, you will communicate those feelings to others.
- They will respond accordingly because they mirror you.
- You will also unintentionally act in such a way as to "sabotage" yourself.
- As a result, you will likely make small-talk failure a self-fulfilling prophecy.

PAST SUCCESS RECOLLECTIONS

Recalling and acknowledging your past successes helps strengthen your Coach. Specifically, it provides your Coach with concrete and specific evidence that you have done things right and well. Thinking of yourself in absolute terms as a "failure" is no longer going to play. You're not a "failure" because you have had successes.

- The more you think about successes, the more successes you will recall having.
- These successes work as part of your disputing your Vulture with facts.

Success Recollection helps you build a bank account of vivid, positive experiences. They are positive experiences you can recall anytime you feel anxious and doubt you can do something. These recollections will help you empower your Coach, dis-empower your Vulture, and create your self-confidence foundation.

When you have a long list of successes at your fingertips to counteract the claim of failure, it becomes harder and harder for you to believe you're a failure or to feel inadequate. You may discount or dismiss them at first as freak occurrences, but the more recollections you compile over time, the more evidence you have and the more confident you can feel. Once again, this is because you will have solid facts that you can do the task—accomplish the goal—and do so effectively, productively, and successfully. You've done it before ... so you can do it again.

Assignment

- Relax yourself in a quiet place, close your eyes, and let your mind drift to times/events/accomplishments in the past—from childhood on to adulthood. Think about when you felt proud and good about yourself. It can be a minor or major incident. It can be about anything to begin with, to get you into that process. But you also will want to find instances of small talk success as well.

✓ For example, think about how you felt when you rode your first two-wheeler; when you first took over a household chore that your mom, dad, or other adult usually did; when you first walked your dog; when you were graduated from school; the time your parent or guardian cried when you did something thoughtful or gave them a special gift. *(Make notes below)*

- As soon as a specific instance comes to mind, I want you to concentrate on it. Absorb the feelings and sensory information. See it, smell it, taste it, touch it, and emotionally feel it. Immerse yourself in the scene and the action.

- You need to recall and observe as clearly as possible what went on, how others responded,

what you thought, and what you felt. You have to
be there in the moment and fully re-experience it.
This means you need to emotionally register every
nuance of the event. See the event - from
beginning to end - as if it were a movie. You're
going to record this in full detail in your Journal.
(Note below)

- In order to create your safe deposit box full of
  Past Success Recollections, you need to stay with
  one recollection until you can play it in your mind
  as a personal movie ... in Technicolor and IMAX,
  until you can pull it up any time you need to
  remind yourself that you have been successful
  and you were proud of yourself. Once you have
  achieved that, you restart the process and locate
  another success event.

- Once you feel comfortable with the process of
  creating and re-living your past successes, you
  can quickly bring your Success Recollection to
  the present. You will start to recall small
  instances of success in interactions with others.
  They can be very minor at first.

- The more aware you are of having had *any*
  conversation successes, the more quickly you will
  become aware of other such success instances.
  Likewise, as you become more familiar with the
  success re-experiencing process, you will be able

to create your success movies more quickly and use them more effectively and efficiently.

- Work on your Past Success Recollections daily and record each recollection in detail in your *Speak Without Fear Daily Journal.*

* * *

A Word of Warning: When you tend to believe you are less than effective in what you do, both in general and in conversations in particular, you may find yourself fighting success remembrances—finding excuses that they weren't really "successes."

It's important to know that initially not being able to conjure up these events is perfectly natural. Over time you will overcome your reluctance to allow yourself to see what you have done that's right and feel good about it.

Chances are good that you have spent a lot of time not being aware of your successes. And when you did become aware of them, you tended to find a way to discount and dismiss them. They didn't seem all *that* important. They didn't fit in with your picture of yourself as "unsuccessful."

Creating Past Success Recollections takes *practice, patience,* and *persistence.* These are the key skills that will make recollection ... and small-talk mastery ... a reality for you.

POISITIVE SELF-TALK

Your Past Success Recollections will support your Positive Self-Talk. By "Positive Self-Talk" I don't mean simple positive affirmations, like, "I'm a great person" or "I can be a success." As I've already indicated, affirmations in that format do NOT work. Why? Because your mind will reject them out of hand, saying, "Yeah, sure, right. Like I really believe that. Get a life!"

Your mind rejects them because they are just wishful thinking. They are abstract and have no weight behind them. However, if you make positive affirmations that are based on the concrete evidence of your Past Success Recollections, your mind will have a harder time discounting and dismissing them. The more success recollections you have, both large and small, the less able your mind will be to disregard your growing repository of success, and the confidence it creates.

Any time an automatic negative thought rears its ugly head, you employ Positive Self-Talk. You point out to yourself that what the negative thoughts are saying isn't true ... you are not a failure because you have succeeded before ... and can prove it!

Furthermore, because you have succeeded before, you can do it *again*. Your Past Success Recollections provide a heavy anchor that keeps you in reality. They keep your thoughts from swirling out of control and into panic, avoidance, and immobility. They start you thinking that maybe you're not so stuck after all ... that just maybe there are success possibilities awaiting you.

Assignment

- Whenever you hear yourself saying, "You can't do that" or "You're a failure" or "You'll never succeed," you need to put up a mental "Stop" sign and pause ... then ask yourself if that is really true. Have you *really* failed at *every single thing* you have ever done? Are you *totally* without skills of any kind?

- Then remind yourself that your Past Success Recollections have shown you that your automatic negative thought is simply *not* true. You have done things well and you have succeeded at tasks, large and small.

- Every time an automatic negative thought occurs, you need to counter its irrationality with the truth. You do it by telling yourself, "That is not true. I have been successful at _____. If I have done it before, I can do it again." Every time your Vulture shoots you down, you need to dispute the validity of what the Vulture says and provide an example to support your claim. No matter how many irrational, inaccurate, fear-oriented, negative things your Vulture says, you will always have one more rational, accurate, and positive arrow in your quiver.

Module 3

Nipping Arousal in the Bud

In Module 1 we looked at why small talk is essential to human interaction and yet so many people have difficulties meeting and conversing with strangers—making small talk.

In Module 2 we noted that working on small talk requires you to look at three distinct areas: Thoughts and Beliefs; Physiological Arousal; and Behavior.

In Module 3 we are going to cover how you can lower your level of physiological arousal. Doing so will help you learn and implement your small-talk skills. It will help you participate more comfortably in every step of the small-talk process and ultimately reap its conversational benefits.

RELAXATION TECHNIQUES

When you're approaching a fearful situation, or already in one such as small talk, typically your heart races and blood pressure rises. You automatically and involuntarily tense your muscles. You breathe more rapidly and shallowly, eliminate too much carbon dioxide, get too much oxygen to your brain, and feel lightheaded. You feel panicky and are ready to flee.

These are the physiological signs we associate with

fear. Experiencing them confirms your initial negative automatic thoughts about making small talk: You have something to fear; you need to act accordingly, and flee.

However, when you do not have these physical signs accompanying your fear thoughts, there is no internal reinforcement of them. It's like viewing a photo of a free tiger versus viewing the real thing free. Generally speaking, when you see a tiger in a photo, there is nothing to confirm that you have to feel afraid of being attacked. As a result, you let any fear thoughts you might have had pass. This means your anxiety cannot and does not take hold.

It's important to remember that your physiology, thoughts, and behaviors are part of a feedback loop so each influences the others and is, in turn, influenced by them. This means that by altering each of the elements you change how they interact in the feedback loop. When you change the interaction, you can change the results.

According to psychologist William James, "The greatest thing then in all education is to make the nervous system our ally instead of our enemy."

The following relaxation techniques are designed to "make your nervous system your ally." These are time-tested strategies for preventing and alleviating your physiological symptoms of small-talk anxiety.

ABDOMINAL BREATHING

Your abdominal breathing is designed to calm you before, during, and after an anxiety-provoking event. This is the primary clinical technique used to address and eliminate panic attacks.

It works both by distracting you from thinking about your body's panic symptoms and by regulating your oxygen-carbon dioxide balance. Specifically, it does so by shifting from shallow upper-lung breathing to lower-lung, diaphragmatic breathing. If you become short of breath at first, stop and take one large breath. Then resume the slow abdominal breathing.

Use the following guidelines:

- Sit in a chair in a quiet room. Place both feet on the floor with one hand on your abdomen and the other on your chest.
- To the count of five, slowly and gently pull in your abdomen (not tightly) as you exhale through your nose. As you do this your chest should remain as still as possible.
- Hold this for three counts (Think "1–2–3").
- Slowly release your belly muscles to the count of five (not moving your chest) and take a small breath.
- Do not fill up your lungs or breathe so hard that your chest moves. (This is one complete diaphragmatic exhalation-inhalation set.)
- Continue breathing in this way, counting "1–2–3" each time for ten breaths.
- Now that you have completed ten breaths, take a moment to see how you feel.

Abdominal Breathing has nothing to do with either deep breathing or shallow breathing. The only determinant of abdominal breathing is that the stomach muscles do the pumping, not the chest muscles. Always begin your breathing exercise with an exhalation.

Assignment

Do Abdominal Breathing at least three times a day. It may take you two to three weeks (or a little longer) to get used to this technique. Consequently, you should be prepared to adapt to it slowly. Your efforts will be rewarded.

VISUALIZATION

Visualization comes in many forms, as we shall see over the duration of this course. One important way it can be used to reduce physiological arousal is to create mini-vacations that provide you a much-needed distraction or break in times of stress. Something like your Past Success recollections, the Visualization is the creation of a highly detailed sensory-based movie, except this movie is of something you find pleasant and relaxing, not something energizing.

It can be a place you like to go, something you like to do, or people you like to be with. Whatever you choose, it must make you want to kick back, let tension go, and enjoy the relaxation, the beauty, or the warmth of human companionship. Narrating what you are experiencing is essential to enhance and reinforce the tension-releasing effect.

It can be as short or as long as you want. It is useful to have multiple-length versions of the same

Visualization and/or several Visualizations of different lengths. This allows you to fit it into different time constraints so time doesn't control you. You control it.

For example, when I want a long Visualization, I picture myself descending a cliff at Torrey Pines State Park in La Jolla, California. I'm making my way to the beach below. As I make my way down the sandy path switchbacks, I notice details about the rocks, plants, and animals I encounter. I tie each detail into my positive feelings and increased state of relaxation. I create a script that is both verbal and graphic and then run my movie whenever I'm feeling stressed.

For a short Visualization (perhaps three minutes), I picture myself floating in my bathtub in my home in Placitas, New Mexico, surrounded by aromatic candles with soft music playing. My eyes are closed and I'm letting all the stress drain away into the warm water as my arms bob and my body rocks gently.

Your mini-vacation can be anywhere from 30 seconds to 5 minutes' long. This means you can use it at a traffic light or at your desk and, *especially, before you go to sleep at night* – whenever or wherever you can use it.

While you might consider using one of your Past Success Recollections as the basis of your Visualization, I recommend you choose something that *reduces* physiological and cognitive arousal rather than activates it. As I've indicated before, Success Recollections are upbeat and geared to energize you and ready you for action. Therefore, if you use your Past Success Recollection at bedtime, it *may* interfere with your sleep.

A relaxing Visualizations requires that you work on it several times a day in order for you to be able to call it up whenever you need it. Then anytime you feel the slightest twinge of stress or anxiety, you can Visualize yourself enjoying and relaxing.

* * *

Some people have difficulty imagining themselves doing things they want to do. As a result, creating even a short movie may be a problem. If you have any difficulty getting into your imagination for this, take a step back and try something neutral and simple, as in the following.

Assignment

- Begin small with something less personal. Close your eyes and picture yourself sitting comfortably in a chair. In your lap is a puppy.
- See the puppy's breed, its color and markings and where they are.
- Feel the puppy's weight on your lap and the loose skin it will grow into.
- Note the puppy's breathing rate. Is it slower or faster than yours?
- Touch the puppy and feel how soft it is.
- Stroke its fur on its head and back. Feel its body wriggle in delight under your touch.
- In your mind's eye see it looking up at you with its soft gaze and puppy smile.
- Continue this image until you can do it comfortably and see, feel, and hear the puppy.
- Once you can do that, take this image one step

further. See yourself walking with the puppy, watching all that the puppy does at the end of its leash.

- When you have this image down, take it a step further to where you are teaching the puppy to chase a ball. See the puppy follow your directions. See the puppy run, catch the ball, and bring the ball back to you. See yourself smiling at it.

- Once you can imagine the puppy, begin working on your personal Visualization again. You'll likely find it easier this time. But don't expect "perfection" all at once. This will take time too.

Starting with Past Success Recollections and working your way toward relaxation Visualizations, you should be able to create any personal Visualization (30-second to even 30-minute) you want.

- Once you master your Visualization skills, you will use the same process to create the movie of your accomplishing your small-talk goals. (We'll discuss this later.)

- You'll need to work on your Visualizations several times a day for at least two weeks in order for you to be able to call it up when you need it.

Assignment

- Create a long and short relaxation Visualization. *(Describe them below)*

- Then use the short version (30-second to 3-minute) at least three times a day.

- Use the longer version (30-minute) once every other day when you carve out a specific time in your schedule in which to do it.

Remember: It's a terrific way to help you relax as you're lying in bed, just before going to sleep. The last thing you will experience before dropping off will be pleasant, comfortable thoughts and feelings.

PHYSICAL EXERCISE

Physical Exercise, in its many forms, has been found clinically to be powerfully effective in reducing both anxiety and depression. It reduces muscle tension and creates an avenue for discharging pent-up frustration. It pumps blood to knotted muscles so they can relax. It increases oxygen circulation to the brain. Moreover, it is thought to stimulate the production of endorphins to increase your sense of well-being. One of the more psychologically beneficial effects is that it shows you a level of control that you have and, further, visibly demonstrates your level of improvement via that control.

While regular, spontaneous movement is necessary to help reduce tension, it often isn't sufficient. You also need extended periods of planned physical activity.

The type of Physical Exercise you choose depends upon your goal. In addition to reducing muscle tension, you can use it for flexibility, strength, cardiovascular conditioning, weight loss, or personal development. It can be done through anaerobic exercise (like isometrics – pitting muscle against muscle in dynamic tension) or aerobic exercise (like swimming, dancing, or playing tennis or basketball). It can be part of a team activity (like baseball) or an individual activity (like weight lifting). It can be done alone (like jogging) or with others (like football). It can be strenuous (like running) or gentle (like walking).

Having several types of exercises to do reduces the likelihood of boredom with exercising. Complementary exercises (anaerobic *and* aerobic) provide balance which is both useful and healthful. Furthermore, Yoga and regular stretching prepares your body for exercise and keeps you limber, especially helping to loosen stress-tightened neck and back muscles which are far too common these days, especially where fear or anxiety occur.

Assignment

- Do one anaerobic or one aerobic exercise once a day for at least 30 minutes per session. What are you going to be doing? *(Note below)*

- Do the anaerobic and aerobic exercises on alternating days. What's your schedule? *(Note below)*

- Do stretching exercises every day—before and after the anaerobic and aerobic exercises. Do them for 20 minutes each day.

Expect that all these arousal-reduction techniques will take three-to-four weeks to have a discernible positive effect. This is because it takes a little bit of time to put positive, functional habits in the place of negative dysfunctional habits. Bad habits may have had up to a lifetime in which to become established so replacing them isn't instantaneous. But by comparison, the change will seem nearly instantaneous.

Additional Arousal-Reduction Recommendations

- Know and accept that these arousal feelings are normal, that your body generates these reactions whenever you are stressed. What makes these feelings seem different is how you think about the symptoms and how you act upon them.

- Be aware that your symptoms are the result of your concern about how others may evaluate you. This is important because it reflects your sensitivity about connecting with others. This sensitivity is good and essential to forming relationships. It should not be discounted or dismissed. Instead, it should be only reduced slightly so you can function more effectively, in order to achieve your small-talk mastery.

- Do not focus or dwell on your arousal symptoms because doing so only makes them more intense and last longer. As a general rule, if you do not reinforce these arousal feelings with fear thoughts or fear actions, they will go away quickly on their own. They are transitory by definition.

- Instead, concentrate on what the other person is saying. You need to get outside yourself and be other-oriented, rather than self-oriented. You can't be anxious about being evaluated negatively when you are focusing on what the other person is saying in normal conversation.

- This means you don't want to focus on what you might respond because it tunes out the speaker. That is, it re-focuses you onto yourself and saying the "right thing." This will tend to make you anxious. Listening is a form of distraction. It is useful and positive for both you and your conversation partner when she or he feels you are paying attention to them.

- Address your symptoms the moment you feel an inkling that they are lurking. Use your Abdominal

Breathing, distract yourself by focusing elsewhere, or find a substitute emotion, such as humor.

- Think of small talk as playing a role for which you need to prepare. You don't want to plunge into this role, or a conversation, cold. Whether you are an actor, athlete, or conversationalist, you benefit from warming up before you perform. "Warming up" for small talk means knowing what to expect and preparing for it.

- Avoid alcohol, antidepressants or tranquilizers whenever possible. Even though they can make interaction more comfortable, they can also become the "reason" you were successful in your small talk. When this happens, you are less likely to give yourself credit for being in control of the situation: "It wasn't my skill, it was the ____." Furthermore, you will likely feel you have to use this "helper" in order to make small talk even possible the next time. You don't want to do anything to take away your sense of personal control. Acknowledgment of your personal control is the foundation of achieving your speaking without fear small-talk goal.

Module 4

Preparing for Small Talk

In Module 3 we looked at the basic ways in which you can reprogram yourself in order to alleviate the physical symptoms of anxiety and substitute relaxation and control. In Module 4 we are going to start building your small-talk foundation.

SMALL-TALK PREPARATION

Successful small talk requires that you learn and understand the nonverbal behaviors that create positive (and negative) interactions. Once you do that, you can become comfortable using them. The primary nonverbal behaviors are eye contact, smiling, and open body orientation. All these precede your uttering a single syllable or word when you encounter someone.

Small-talk strategies do not exist in a vacuum. They are interpreted and expressed by you. When you express them, you do so with verbal and nonverbal behavior. We're going to talk about nonverbal behavior first.

NONVERBAL BEHAVIOR

Most of your interpersonal communication and interaction is guided by nonverbal behaviors. The meaning of these actions can be in the behavior itself or how it is performed. Nonverbal behaviors are exceedingly important, accounting for up to 80% of the actual communication.

Why are nonverbal behaviors important? While we rely upon words for our communication, our body language is much more revealing and powerful. It's powerful because it is instinctively absorbed. We can feel its meaning in our gut. Moreover, it taps into a depth of feeling and does so quickly. Words, on the other hand, are symbols of ideas and concepts that we have to take the time to mentally translate.

Nonverbal behavior tends to be spontaneous. That is, many of these actions are automatic and unintentional. Unlike words, they are unconscious, involuntary, and less likely to be manipulated.

According to body language researcher Paul Ekman, nonverbal behavior is universal. While words in each language means specific things to speakers of that language, body language can be understood across cultures because it relates to shared human experience about basic aspects of life. You can smile, grimace, furrow your brow in anger, or scrunch your face in sadness and everyone will know what you mean.

What can nonverbal behaviors tell you and others? They can tell you, for example, how well a joke is going over. If the smile to the punch line takes place in the lower part of the face (like, upwardly-curved lips but no eye crinkling), you can immediately sense that the joke had only a lukewarm reception. The response you're receiving is polite and detached. If, on the other hand, the response is with an open mouth smile, wide-open or totally crinkled eyes, and with lots of body involvement, you can immediately sense the enthusiasm and appreciation for a clever joke or one well-told.

What is important to know is that there are certain nonverbal behaviors that are consistently associated with people who are successful. When you use these behaviors, you will give off the aura of someone who is successful and confident. As you incorporate them into your own behavioral repertoire, others will respond to them—and you—positively, like a reflection in a mirror. This is true for almost any situation, whether personal or work-related.

CONFIDENCE-SIGNALING BEHAVIORS

- Good eye contact
- Squaring your body to the person to whom you're speaking
- Standing erect with shoulders back and pelvis forward
- Chin thrust upward
- Firm handshake
- Striding when walking
- Slight smile
- Keeping gestures minimal and from the elbow (no flailing arms)
- Willing to engage in conversations and leading them
- Good listener
- No hand-to-face gestures, covering mouth or nose or head scratching
- No repetitive, non-essential body gestures

- Dressing conservatively and appropriately for business or the occasion, no flamboyant or faddish trends
- Open positions with arms and legs.

EYE CONTACT

Eye contact is very powerful. It opens and closes the lines of communication and regulates the flow. It conveys emotion and signals interest or disinterest. It demonstrates confidence and power.

Confident and powerful people make eye contact to show interest in communication. A small smile reinforces their interest in interacting and displays friendliness. After they start to speak, they look away to maintain the speaking role. They then look back when they are finished to signal that they are done. They may conclude with a slight smile.

If, however, what they are saying takes longer than two-to-three minutes, they will tend to glance back at their listener to check to see if the listener is listening, then look away again until they finish their turn.

WHY IS EYE CONTACT IMPORTANT?

Of all the behaviors in our interpersonal communication toolbox eye communication is one of the most important. This is because of all of our communication behaviors, which include eye contact, posture/movement, gestures, facial expression, dress/appearance, and voice intonation, it is *only* our eyes which make a direct connection with other people.

Eye contact carries messages of the *three I's*:

Involvement, Intimacy, and Intimidation. Furthermore, the only thing that separates involvement from intimacy and intimidation is the duration of the eye contact.

Involvement represents over 90% of our personal communication (excluding telephone, iPhone, cell phone, e-mail, social media, and blogging use). When our eyes meet for two-to-five seconds, it shows our interest, enthusiasm, excitement, and empathy.

Intimacy and intimidation are emotionally and behaviorally opposite, but both involve looking from over ten seconds to two or more minutes. The actual meaning of the long connection is usually interpreted by other body language, the context of the situation, and the relationship of the people involved.

You should look at each person naturally, looking away occasionally so you don't appear to stare. But you have to be careful not to look as if you're darting your eyes. That is, you don't want to move your eyes around rapidly. When you do, you tend to look like a frightened animal or as if you're hiding something.

Likewise, looking at the floor, out the window, or any place except at the other person makes you look uncomfortable and disinterested. You need to look directly at the person (at least close to their eye area— one eye or the other, bridge of the nose, between the eyes, high on the cheek, an eyebrow. Anything other than looking at the person's face will tend to make the other person uncomfortable.

Another eye behavior that conveys disinterest or lack of interest is the slow blink. You've seen people who do it. In general, your blinks are instantaneous. But slow-blinkers close their eyes and don't open them for at least five seconds. Our impression of them is that perhaps they're bored or nervous. Which one it is specifically doesn't really matter. What does matter is that they appear not to want to be where they are with you.

I had a "computer date" who was a slow blinker. He closed his eyes to talk about himself and closed them even when I managed to get a word in edge-wise. I felt invisible, angry, insulted, and confused. It left me wondering was he always like this? Was this his specific response to me? Was he so anxious that he couldn't bring himself to look at me as he talked? He said he was a physician. Really? I hoped he was in research instead of handling patients. When he did momentarily look at me, I'm sure my furrowed brow and my head cocked to the side didn't spur him on to consider contacting me again.

INCREASING YOUR AWARENESS OF EYE COMMUNICATION

It is imperative that you increase your awareness and develop your eye communication skills.

Assignment

- Observe others in real life and on TV/movies to see how different eye contact makes you feel about the person or character. What did you observe? *(Note below)*

- Videotape yourself talking with and listening to another or have a friend unobtrusively monitor and analyze your eye-contact habits. What did you discover? *(Note below)*

In your *Speak Without Fear Daily Journal* you need to record what you discovered from this taping or the friend's verbal summarization of your nonverbal behavior.

You need to keep in mind that your eyes speak volumes about you to others. They tell:

- Who you are
- What you are
- What is meaningful to you
- Your level of relaxation
- Your acceptance of others
- Your sincerity and trustworthiness.

With awareness and practice you can make them say what you want when you want them to.

DEVELOPING EYE COMMUNICATION SKILLS

To develop your eye communication skills you need to expose yourself very gradually to having extended eye contact with another. That is, you start small and continue to build on each subsequent success as detailed below.

Assignment

- Start by giving yourself a daily target number of people with whom you are going to make eye contact. *(Note your number below)*

- Start with people you know. Make eye contact with them for two seconds. How did that work for you? *(Note below)*

- If in a week's time you have met your target number, add two strangers to the number for the next week. How did that work for you? *(Note below)*

- As you get comfortable, each week introduce another stranger to your target number. How did that work for you? *(Note below)*

- In your *Speak Without Fear Daily Journal* you need to record from your notes below:

- ✓ What you expected to happen when you made eye contact *(Note below)*

- ✓ What thoughts you had before you made eye contact *(Note below)*

- ✓ What actually happened when you made it *(Note below)*

- ✓ How you felt afterward *(Note below)*

Module 5

What Image Are You Presenting?

SMILING ISN'T JUST ABOUT WHITE TEETH

Your smile is your most important facial expression. When it is spontaneous, it warms people. It indicates interest and willingness to talk. It inspires confidence, trust, and understanding.

However, that isn't to say you should smile all the time. Anything done to excess loses its power to have the desired effect. When smiling is overdone, it tends to create the impression of someone who is submissive and trying desperately to be accepted and liked. It can also suggest that you're trying to be very "friendly" in a sexual sense.

Smiling plus eye contact establishes sincerity and emphasizes a point in conversation. Smiling—unlike any other facial gesture—has the power to reward others. If someone is listening attentively to you and you smile and briefly gaze at them, you will encourage them to continue their positive listening behavior.

Assignment

Once you are comfortable making eye contact for two seconds, you are ready to add a small smile. Of course, be circumspect about at whom you smile. When females smile at male strangers for an extended period of time, those males will likely take it as a come on. Everything should be in moderation and according to the dictates of the environment.

In your *Speak Without Fear Daily Journal* you need to record

- What did you expect to happen? *(Note below)*

- What thoughts did you have before you made eye contact and smiled, and then? *(Note below)*

- What actually happened when you made it? *(Note below)*

- How did you feel afterward? *(Note below)*

A NOD TO NODDING

Nodding is a seemingly trivial and little recognized behavior exhibited by listeners. What makes it important is that it lets speakers know that they are being listened to. It also suggests there is understanding and, perhaps, some degree of agreement with what is being said.

When there is no nonverbal feedback, speakers tend to assume that the listener is disinterested, confused, or even in disagreement. A slow stream of small nods signals understanding. A single nod may signal agreement. And a series of rapid nods generally means the listener is impatient to speak.

Assignment

Whenever in a conversation, you need to become aware of your nodding behavior.

- Consciously nod slowly and occasionally. How does the speaker respond? *(Note below)*

- After that, Nod only in agreement. How does the speaker respond? *(Note below)*

- Finally nod rapidly. How does the speaker respond? *(Note below)*

- Record your observations in your *Speak Without Fear Daily Journal.*

BODY POSTURE AND ORIENTATION

Your posture reveals how you think of both yourself and the listener. If you slouch, with your head down talking to your feet, you will look as if you don't hold yourself in very high regard. Your listener won't feel you hold him or her in high regard either. He or she will rapidly decide not to continue to talk to you.

However, if you stand straight and tall with your shoulders back, you will look confident and competent. You will also look welcoming and interested.

Your body orientation publicly demonstrates your availability for interaction. When your arms and legs are crossed or close to your body, your position is closed. When you are leaning back or looking away, your position is closed. This orientation says you are not available. You may even be angry or hostile. So, "Buzz off."

But, when your arms and legs are apart comfortably, when you are leaning forward, facing the other person, or making eye contact, your position is open. You are available and interested. You look and feel welcoming. So, "Come on down!"

Assignment

- Whenever you can, catch yourself, full body if possible, in a mirror or on any reflective surface. Are you standing tall, shoulders and head back, walking briskly or standing in an open position, and looking confident and friendly OR are you hunkered over, round shouldered, shuffling along or standing in a closed position, and looking unsure and unfriendly? *(Note below)*

- When it's possible, have a close friend or trusted family member monitor and record your body orientation. Have them do it at times when you are unaware of their presence or actions. It is imperative that you be able to "observe" your own behavior in some way. What did you discover? *(Note below)*

- Look at people who look confident, alert, enthusiastic, and open to interaction. How do they hold themselves? Make a note specifically of *what* they do and *how* they do it. This may take time. What did you discover? *(Note below)*

- Then put yourself in their shoes and practice their behaviors that demonstrate confidence. Do it at least once a day first by yourself to get used to what you're doing. Then do it in front of others, especially others who have seen you before. How did they react? What did you discover? *(Note below)*

- In your *Speak Without Fear Daily Journal* you need to record where you are starting, what you are doing, and each small change you make.

PERSONAL SPACE

Personal space is the distance between participants in conversation. It acts as a buffer zone. The space will contract or expand depending upon the situation and people involved. In general, for impersonal business-like contact the preferred space is 4+-to-12 feet. For more personal interactions, with close friends and acquaintances, the preferred space is 1.5-to-4 feet.

However, you need to be aware that this will vary by culture. Some cultures prefer a smaller distance and some prefer a larger one. It can create some awkwardness when there is a personal space mismatch.

This is where one person keeps stepping closer as the other person keeps stepping back. When only one small-talk participant is aware of this difficulty, there tends to be little you can do to resolve it perfectly. A comfortable compromise is often the best you can hope for. But if you know ahead of time the other person is from a different culture or country, try to check out, on Google or Bing, etc., what the etiquette rules are for her or his culture's personal space.

Assignment

- Watch people in conversations and note their distance from one another. What did you discover? Does age, sex, or nationality seem to make a difference? *(Note below)*

- Watch what happens as strangers approach one another. They likely will do what's called the "diplomat's waltz" as they try to establish a mutually acceptable distance for the interaction. What did you discover? Does age, sex, or nationality seem to make a difference? *(Note below)*

- Determine how the distances you personally prefer differ from when you're talking with those close to you to when you're talking with those who are strangers. What did you discover? Does age, sex, or nationality seem to also make a difference? *(Note below)*

- Record this in your *Speak Without Fear Daily Journal.*

TO TOUCH OR NOT TO TOUCH

Touch is a "touchy" nonverbal behavior. This is because it breaches personal space, suggests intimacy, and has sexual connotations. Some people are touch-ers and emphasize their words and emotion by touching the other person, but not necessarily with sexual undertones. Women touching men can send confusing signals about the underlying intent. Men touching women can also send confusing signals because it is often a demonstration of dominance. Women, in general, find the touch uncomfortable unless they have a close relationship.

Some people may not like being touched by strangers, irrespective of the intent, because they are shy or socially anxious. It can make them feel uneasy, self-conscious, anxious, or angry. As a result, even if you are a "touching person," it is generally better not to touch stranger at all or until you have evidence it probably won't be misinterpreted. And, if you do touch, do so *very* cautiously, touching only the hand or lower arm. Legs, upper torso, head, and face are out of bounds.

Assignment

- Observe people in conversations to see who touches whom and under what circumstances. What did you discover? Does age, sex, nationality, or situation seem to make a difference? *(Note below)*

- How do people in social gatherings or in public tend to respond to the touching? What did you discover? Does age, sex, nationality, situation, or location seem to make a difference? *(Note below)*

- How do you respond to touching? What did you discover? Does age, sex, nationality, situation, or location seem to make a difference? (*Note below*)

- Record this in your *Speak Without Fear Daily Journal.*

COMMUNICATING SINCERITY AND TRUSTWORTHINESS

What's the first thing you notice about another person? It's their physical appearance and body language. Before they utter a single syllable or word, you have made a tentative assessment of them. It's tentative because you really need patterns of behavior and appearance over time in order to reliably predict how a person is likely to think, feel, and act.

Sincerity is an attribute we all want to communicate to others with whom we interact in order to have them like you. Sincerity can also enable you to get what you want from the interaction. Therefore, you want to be seen as natural, free of artifice, honest, and genuine. Authentic.

Sincerity begets trust, and trust makes people feel comfortable. Sincerity and trust are the keystones of any interaction or relationship, whether with your doctor, significant other, boss, or local car dealer.

When you experience anxiety in social situations, you may send out signals that others may misinterpret because they look like other things. For example, if you tend to stand at a greater-than-average physical distance from others, the behavior may be seen as a sign of arrogance. But if you're aware of the impression you want to make and what components make up that impression, you can counteract negative impressions and create positive ones.

For example, you can stand a little closer than you normally would. You can show your openness in others ways (like open stance, smiling, eye contact) while still standing where you normally would. In other words, you can play a role that will accomplish what you want.

In order to appear sincere and trustworthy with others, you need to concentrate on two categories of nonverbal behavior: humility and openness.

THERE'S A LOT TO BE SAID ABOUT HUMILITY

Humility is the recognition that people have value and no one has more or less value because of one's status. Unlike arrogant people who try to separate themselves from others by rank, humble individuals tend to be less overly competitive and more forgiving, compassionate, and understanding. Nonverbal behaviors associated with humility include:

- Quiet demeanor—not boastful, flamboyant, and boisterous
- Focusing on others rather than on oneself
- Self-deprecating humor
- Attention to courtesy
- Listening with head nodding and use of acknowledging sounds like "uh-huh"
- Turn-taking in conversations.

However, like anything, humility can become a detriment when taken to extreme. People with self-presentation- and self-promotion anxiety tend to do that because they lack self-confidence and don't want to make themselves the center of attention.

HUMILITY DOESN'T MEAN NOT TOOTING YOUR OWN HORN

Having humility does NOT mean that you cannot or

should not let others know about your abilities, skills, and successes. While this is true in general, it is especially true with respect to the work place.

Whether you are looking for a job or promotion, it is essential that you know how to share your experiences and resources with decision makers. As much as you may wish it, your work simply cannot speak for itself. Only you know what you had to do to produce that particular result: What abilities, how much innovation, leadership, and bottom-line-related skills were involved.

It's NOT bragging to share this important data because it gives you visibility and credibility and separates you from others candidates for the job or promotion.

There are many ways to provide this information to those who matter. One approach is to present it in anecdotes. An anecdote is a short interesting, even amusing, story about an incident or person and follows a particular format.

Starting with a topic sentence to introduce the story, you would briefly describe the background of the problem to be solved, what action you took, and what results your solution produced. Whenever possible, you'd want to present the result quantitatively and related to what contributes to the bottom-line: Making money, saving money, saving time, etc.

For example, interviewers invariable ask you to "Tell me about yourself." I was being considered for a consulting job that had creative elements so I decided to start with my creativity:

"I've done a number of things I consider creative. One example is when I worked on a pharmaceutical advertising campaign where the company's promotional materials to surgeons had failed to get the response they wanted.

"I researched that market, ran focus groups, and discovered that the ads didn't emphasize what the physicians considered the primary benefit of the ophthalmic ointment during surgery. Therefore, I developed ads that emphasized targeting the vulnerable eye with supportive text. Within six months surgeons' use of the eye ointment increased by 20%."

This same format is useful in regular small talk as well. People in all sorts of situations will often ask you what you do. This T-BAR formula can make your response simpler and easier to remember what you want to say. Because you are speaking about what you did, a problem and your related problem-solving behaviors, and not about yourself personally or emotionally, you can present it more analytically and objectively.

Of course, if you're *not* speaking with a company interviewer or decision maker, you can omit the results achieved and provide them only if asked about them. In social conversations, the other person's next question about you would likely be about your results so your being prepared with an answer is a good move as well.

Topic sentence

Background of problem

Action taken for solution

Result achieved

T-BAR helps you convey what you want to communicate in the most efficient and effective way possible.

NECESSITY OF OPENNESS

Openness is exposing yourself, to some degree, in your behavior and speech so that others can begin to get to know and understand you. Nonverbal behaviors associated with openness include:

- Fully facing the person when speaking or listening
- Eyes open and arms uncrossed
- Hands are kept away from the mouth and off of the hips
- Standing 2-3 feet from the other person but not invading her/his personal space
- Warm, relaxed smile with frequent and prolonged eye contact
- Contributing to the conversation but not trying to be the center of it all.

Module 6

What You Can Learn from Others

From others you can observe and learn the different ways to relax, what comfortable looks like, how people express confidence, and how they navigate conversations. In particular, you can find role models.

WHAT ARE ROLE MODELS?

Role models are people whom you admire or respect and whom you'd like to emulate in some fashion. You can admire them for their accomplishments, attitude, specific nonverbal behaviors, the way they speak, their assertiveness, ... the list goes on. They are important for your finding identification with successful others, creating hope, seeking resources, and gaining confidence. There are role models all around you. One person may have all that you want to identify with. A number of people may have different individual behaviors or attitudes you want to emulate. You can have as many role models as you need. Of course, having one with everything would be preferable but, unfortunately, is sometimes hard to find.

MODELING NONVERBAL BEHAVIOR

One of the interesting things about playing a role that represents what you'd like to be is that over time you are likely to become it. You will tend to develop a habit of these positive behaviors and simply incorporate them naturally into your own behavioral repertoire.

Doing this does NOT make you an "imposter"! You're not trying to be something you're not. You're taking on and practicing qualities and skills that you value. You're trying on behaviors that other people respond favorably to. You're only taking on positive behaviors that fit with your overall personality. You do this unconsciously all the time anyway because you want to try new thing and improve yourself. It's just in this situation you're doing it consciously.

Doing this is easier and more comfortable because that someone you admire has already done it ... and done it successfully. You have a template to follow. As a result, there is less risk and uncertainty about whether you are doing it correctly. You just observe and emulate them the way it suits you best.

And before you know it, these behaviors become part of you—how you think and feel and respond. As your behaviors change, your attitudes are likely to change to support them, making these positive behaviors doubly rewarding.

Assignment

Ask yourself the following:

- Who are people (3-to-5) you admire for their small talk confidence and conversational ability? (These can be people you know, well-known personalities, characters in a book, play, movie, or on TV, or some combination of these.) These need to be people you can observe.

- *Note:* If you cannot observe your role model repeatedly to do your analysis, you may find it helpful to use a character in a movie where you can replay the behaviors of interest, or one on a weekly TV series. Why did you pick these specific people? *(Note below)*

- Observe them as often as possible in order to answer these questions fully.

- What is there about them specifically in the small-talk context that you find appealing? *(Note below)*

- How do they achieve their small-talk smoothness? Specifically, is it:

- What they say (content—their introduction, small talk strategies, topic categories, type of self-disclosure)? We'll talk more about this later on. *(Note below)*

- How they say it (their tone, inflection, attitude) *(Note below)*

- What they do to make it interpersonal (listening, turn- taking behaviors, bringing out best in the other person) *(Note below)*

- How they use nonverbal behavior (eye contact, smiling, body movement, touching, gestures, personal space, and body positions) to create smoothness, show confidence, and make the interaction comfortable? *(Note below)*

- How would you describe their style? *(Note below)*

- How could you achieve the same thing? *(Note below)*

- Once you have a detailed list of what your role models do that you want to emulate, record this in your *Speak Without Fear Daily Journal.*

DESIGN THE ROLE YOU WANT TO PLAY

Once you have made note of the specific nonverbal behaviors your role models use, you will then design the role you want to play. Your role is made of the characteristic behaviors you want to put on and try out.

You need to put yourself in your role model's skin—mentally in their shoes—and ask how they would think and act in your situation. (*Remember:* If they look confident, they probably feel confident). You, then, act and feel as if you were that person, or as if you were in a movie about them. You do what they would do and assume their attitude.

Assignment

- You need to carry index cards around with you that list your role models' nonverbal behaviors. Each card represents a specific nonverbal behavior. For example, you might list the following introductory small talk behaviors—one per card: Open body position, smile, eye contact, and comfortable personal space.

- You will rehearse each behavior in private before you practice the behavior in public. Your public schedule is as follows:

- Day #1 you work on the first index card behavior, practicing it at least three times a day. What behavior did you choose? How did it go? What did you feel? *(Note below)*

- Day #2 you work the second index card behavior, practicing it at least three times a day. What behavior did you choose? How did it go? What did you feel? *(Note below)*

- Go through all four cards.

- Day #5 you combine the first and second behaviors: For example, you show open body position and smile, which you practice at least three times a day. What behavior did you choose? How did it go? What did you feel? *(Note below)*

- It's important that each day you carefully note how it feels to you AND its nonverbal behavioral impact on the other person. The effect your behavior has on you may seem very slight initially and may not be easy to detect right away. What you're creating is confidence behaviors. You need to think of each of them as a space suit you can slip into any time you want you want to explore and discover your outer space.

- You continue this process until you can comfortably do the full sequence of behaviors: That is, in a social situation you stand with an open body position, smile, make eye contact, and establish a comfortable personal space with those who approach or whom you approach. What behaviors did you use together? How did it go? What was the other person's nonverbal response? What did you feel? *(Note below)*

As you become more comfortable employing your role models' introductions, strategies, topic categories, and self-disclosure methods, you will be creating templates and small- talk scripts of your own.

You may feel a little detached at first. But don't worry. That's normal. You are consciously acting on what is generally an unconscious behavior ... so it's likely to feel awkward. But that won't last long. When you find it working for you, you will attach yourself to it and make it your own.

Remember. This is how you learn what works for you, what fits your goals and values and will accomplish what you want. This is how you expand your behavioral repertoire to meet new situations. This is how you grow and develop. You're developing your skills and making strides toward reaching your small-talk potential.

GETTING INTO THE SKIN OF YOUR ROLE MODEL

There are numbers of ways to get into the skin of your role model.

- *Visualization* is one. You need to envision yourself as the other person in the specific social situations that you will or want to find yourself in. You need to envision yourself as the other person confidently doing the things they do and saying the things they say.

- *Videotaping* is another. As already mentioned, you need to see yourself doing the new behaviors so you can tailor them to your personality. You want the new behaviors to have a custom, comfortable fit.

- *Tape recording* yourself is also beneficial. What works particularly well is recording yourself making your introduction, asking a question, and making a comment as you would normally do it. Then, you record yourself as your role model, making the same introduction, asking a question, and making a comment but with the role model's behaviors, attitude, and confidence.

Listening to both recordings can be enlightening. Aside from probably not liking to hear the sound of your own voice, you may find that what you say normally is not as bad as you thought it was. You may find that the distance between what you have been doing and what you want to do is not so great after all ... that it would take only a little practice to "be" your role model in attitude and behavior.

Repeatedly listening to these recordings can help you find the right tone and inflection that makes you sound as positive, pleasant, and approachable as possible. If you use a movie or TV character as one of your role models, you can play and replay the character's speech patterns as often as you need to. When watching the movie or TV show, you can even act out what the person is doing along with them.

Keep in mind that if there be a small-talk behavior you feel is important but you don't feel comfortable doing it exactly the way your role models do it, you can use what they do as a springboard. That is, you can personalize it, make it fit your own style without changing its impact significantly. The goal is to maintain the core or essence of the behavior, not necessarily the behavior itself as portrayed precisely by the role model.

This is what actor Cary Grant did. Born into poverty in the Cockney section of London, he worked as a stilt-walker but wanted to better himself. He decided to become an actor. But not *just* an actor, he had a particular persona in mind. He wanted to be seen as one who was sophisticated, cultured, refined, suave, and confident.

Consequently, he dressed the part and acted the part. He modeled himself after those who had the qualities and characteristics he desired. Over time he worked his way into the role and became the part ... and the epitome of the handsome leading man ideal of his movie era on and off the screen.

Module 7

Creating Your Small-Talk Plan

Doing your Abdominal Breathing, Visualization, and Positive Self-Talk based on your Past Success Recollections is necessary. Practicing your eye contact and smiling is necessary. But they aren't sufficient. You still need to construct a Plan for each small-talk event you encounter.

PREPARATION MEANS EVENT PLANNING

Your Plan includes what your goal is for the small-talk interaction(s) and what you need to do to achieve that goal. That is, you must *concretely* and *specifically* determine the step-by-step process you will go through to successfully meet your goal in each situation.

Unfortunately, your small-talk mastery does not happen just because of your doing a few relaxation exercises, reprogramming your thinking, and learning how to make eye contact and smile. It is also the result of your making a systematized, step-by-step, and concerted effort to make it happen. Your preparation is the name of the game.

WHAT SHOULD THE PLAN INCLUDE?

- Knowing in detail the reason for/purpose of the

event.

- Being sincere, positive, and in the moment.
- Asking open-ended questions, such as *how*, *what*, *why*, and *to what degree.*
- Being a good listener—not thinking about yourself or what you are going to say next, but what you can contribute to the conversation as the other person finishes.
- Determining what you want to learn from each small talk partner and sharing some information about yourself.
- Acting like a host and not a guest.
- Exiting conversations and the event gracefully and comfortably.
- Assessing to what degree you achieved your goal.
- Praising and rewarding yourself for your effort and whatever results you achieved.

We will be covering these areas in depth shortly.

REWARD LIST

As you are making progress in your thoughts, feelings, beliefs, and behaviors, it is essential that you reward yourself in a more formal fashion. Your progress demands to be rewarded.

Now instead of just feeling good about a successful situation (no matter whether large or small), you are to physically *pat yourself on the back* and *say aloud* (when you can) your Reward Statement:

"That was a success. I am proud of myself for doing

that. I knew I could do it. Everyday I'm getting more and more successful at small talk. This feels really good."

Then you need to make up a list of graded rewards from which to choose so that you actually reinforce your having done something positive. You have to show yourself that you know and believe that you deserve to feel good about your accomplishment. Rewards can be anything that you like.

The Reward List can run from something as small as a few-minutes' break or a candy bar to taking yourself out to dinner or getting yourself something you have wanted. You have to decide what type of reward best fits what success.

But each success, *no matter how small*, <u>requires</u> a reward. The reward you choose for each and every success should be commensurate with the level of the success. The overriding thought should be, "I've done something important and I deserve to be rewarded for it!"

Assignment

- Create your Reward List and put it on an index card you carry with you. What things small and large do you find rewarding? But don't make it all about food. *(Note below)*

- Create an index card to carry with you that reminds you of the three-step Reward Process: 1. Pat yourself on the back; 2. Make the reward statement; and 3. Give yourself a reward.

- Be sure to memorize your Reward Statement: "That was a success. I am proud of myself for doing that. I knew I could do it. Everyday I'm getting more and more successful at small talk. This feels really good." And carry it on an index card with you as well. This is further sensory and cognitive reinforcement. Yes, it's that important!

HOW TO CREATE YOUR EVENT PLAN

You start by thinking of an event (large or small) in which you would like to be making small talk. With it in mind you lay out a Plan for yourself that follows the Preparation Steps below. You really need to write this out on paper and not try to simply hold it in your head. Your memory can unconsciously change from your original plan but a hard copy of it won't.

Assignment

Ask Yourself the Following Questions:

- What is the reason for/purpose of the event? *(Note below)*

- Who will be there and why? *(Note below)*

- What do you have in common with them? *(Note below)*

- Why are you going to be there? *(Note below)*

- What benefits can you achieve by being there? *(Note below)*

- To what degree are you generally up on current events? *(Note below)*

- What will you say in introducing yourself? *(Note below)*

- How, when, and where will you meet others at the event? *(Note below)*

Next list the following Preparation Steps on several index cards. This is the sequence of behaviors you need to perform at the event while making small talk.

- Making eye contact and smiling.
- Repeating the other person's name.
- Being sincere, positive, and in the moment.
- Asking open-ended questions, such as *how*, *what, why*, and *to what degree*, and/or making comments.
- Being a good listener—not thinking about yourself or what you are going to say next, but what you can contribute to the conversation as the other person finishes.
- Determining what you want to learn from each small talk partner and sharing some information about yourself.
- Acting like a host and not a guest.
- Exiting conversations and the event gracefully and comfortably.
- Assessing to what degree you achieved your goal.
- Praising and rewarding yourself for your effort and whatever results you achieved using your Reward List and the three-step Reward Process.

VISUALIZING PARTICIPATING IN THE EVENT

After you create your Plan, you need to *visualize* yourself actually going through the steps:

- Preparing for the event

- Arriving at it
- Introducing yourself
- Meeting people
- Making conversation.

At each step you need to see yourself acting positively, creating a positive impression on others, and coming away feeling proud of your efforts and results.

Short visualizations tend to be easier to do than longer ones. Therefore, you may want to start with the first behavior in your sequence and be able to imagine it fully before going on to the next in the sequence.

For some people it works well to do each individual behavior in the sequence and then go back and begin to combine them. You would do the first and second together and when that feels comfortable, you would add the third. And so on, creating a chain of the behaviors you will follow.

Assignment

- Work on the individual behaviors every day for one week. How did it go? *(Note below)*

- Work on the sequence of behaviors every day for one week. How did it go? *(Note below)*

- Visualize these steps in sequence at least once a day. How did it go? *(Note below)*

- Record all of this in your *Speak Without Fear Daily Journal* for every event.

Assignment

In your *Speak Without Fear Daily Journal* go to a new page and break down what achieving your conversation goal actually entails behaviorally. That is, what *specifically* and *concretely* do you personally need to do in order to achieve your own particular goal. Use the questions and your notes here for it.

- What is your goal? List *all* the steps (actions) involved in your Plan toward that goal. *(Note below)*

- What you have achieved so far toward that goal. *(Note below)*

- Note what you still need to do to achieve the goal. *(Note below)*

- Ask yourself what positive things will happen as you accomplish each new step. Be as detailed as possible. *(Note below)*

✓ How will you feel?

✓ How will others respond?

✓ How will you reward yourself for each successful step?

- Ask yourself what positive things have already occurred as you have accomplished your beginning steps. *(Note below)*

Module 8

Initial Small Talk Strategies

In the previous module we talked about preparing for every small-talk interaction. Preparation builds your confidence level. When you're prepared, you can kiss panic good-bye. The reason is that you don't have to suddenly search for something, anything to say. Instead, you already have something on the tip of your tongue. This allows you to comfortably proceed and concentrate on the actual conversation.

Anticipating what things will be like and *loosely scripting* what you might say in the situation also provides you a way of knowing what to expect. Your Small-Talk Plan Visualization further enhances that. Knowing what to expect likewise removes a great deal of the risk and anxiety from the situation.

In Module #8 we're going to cover icebreakers and other templates and strategies for starting conversations.

ICEBREAKERS

Icebreakers are what you immediately say when you approach someone to start a conversation. What you will say is something about which you need to think about ahead of time, plan, and script. You don't want to leave this to chance.

Remember: If you do not know what to expect and are not prepared, anxiety will likely sever the connection between your brain and tongue, obliterating your memory and your ability to speak smoothly, clearly, and coherently. It will leave you struggling to say anything, much less anything you want to say.

But before you say a word, however, you need to start with a *smile* and *2 seconds of eye contact.*

INITIATION STRATEGIES

In general, the best ways to initiate small talk is by

- Making a comment
- Asking a question (open-ended whenever possible)
- Ending you comment with a question which will put the ball in the other person's court and start the small-talk interaction.

BASIC SMALL-TALK INITIATOR TOPICS

There are four categories of Basic Small-Talk Topics:

- *Event, circumstance or activity* in which you both find yourselves

- *Environment* (weather, what's going in the news that's neutral, location of the event, or the actual physical environs of the event)

- *Other person* (name, accent, appearance, non-sexual physical attributes, attire, belongings, skills, event- or environmentally-related interests, movies, books, music, etc.)

- *Yourself* (thoughts, feelings, interests, activities, skills, attributes, current situation, event- or environmentally-related interests, movies, books, music, etc.)

When you know something about the event and/or environment, you will automatically have something in common with the person with whom you are speaking. When you positively and sincerely refer to attributes of the other person, you automatically create a positive impression and emotional bond.

Relating an amusing little anecdote about the event or environment also creates a smooth introduction to a conversation. What makes this work especially well is if it is humorous, semi-personal, and identifiable. This means everyone is likely to be able to relate to it in some way.

For example, "The last time I was here my cell phone kept beeping at me because the battery was low but I thought it was someone else's phone. I kept grimacing and looking around for the annoying offender. And it was me!"

COMBINING INITIATING STRATEGIES WITH BASIC TOPICS

Here are a few examples of what initiators look like:

- Event Comment – "They have a good band here."

- Event Question – "How often does this band play here?"
- Environment Comment – "The forecast didn't mention golf ball-size hail."
- Environment Question – "How often does the weather act like this here?"
- Other Person Comment – "Your pashmina reminds me of fine Irish lace."
- Other Person Question – "How did you acquire that beautiful shawl?"
- Yourself Comment – "I really liked the author's book about cloning."
- Yourself Comment – "I sometimes play with a pick-up band like this one."

It does NOT matter if the comment or question isn't brilliant or witty. It doesn't have to be. In fact, it isn't expected to be. All it has to do let the other person know you're interested ... and let you know if the other person is open to having a conversation with you.

Think of it as a key to open a door. If you deliver the comment or question positively, authentically, and respectfully, you significantly enhance your chances that the person will be receptive ... and the key will fit the lock.

INTRODUCING YOURSELF

Depending upon the formality of the situation, you may extend your hand in a firm handshake. But in more casual circumstances, you may just say, "Hello, I'm ___" (your name) and something very brief about you.

The brief thing you say about yourself should be descriptive of what you do in your work or personal life or what your interests are. For example, when referring to what you do, it is generally better not to simply label yourself: "I'm an electrical engineer (coach, bus driver, corporate vice president, or mother)." This is because it leaves the other person with little information with which to work. As a result, it is less likely they will have an easy springboard from which to respond. Being left with a response of "Oh, really" Or "Oh, isn't that interesting. I've never met a ____ before" frequently doesn't get you very far.

Instead, you want to say something that's intriguing (perhaps humorous) that describes

- What you do under your job label
- What you like to do outside of work.

Under the job label, for example,

- The electrical engineer might say, "I helped keep NASA's Shuttle from burning up upon re-entry."
- The coach might say, "I help individuals achieve work-life satisfaction the fastest way possible."
- The bus driver might say, "I help keep the city moving efficiently and commuters save gas."
- A mother might say, "I juggle transportation for educational and sporting activities."

You want to speak in terms of your work or *activity process*, NOT its category label.

You can be as creative as you like. While you want to

transmit information to the other person, you also want to intrigue them enough to want to find out more about you. Saying any of the above with a slight smile, as if what you're saying is tongue in cheek, can add to the intrigue

Under your interests, you can use your activities and hobbies as the focal point. This is especially useful if it relates to the current situation (although it does *not* have to).

For example,

- At a sports or health-related event one might say, "In trying to keep fit, I'm preparing to run in the Boston Marathon next year."

- In a pet-related situation one might say, "My old Lab, Barnaby, and I are getting ready for the city-wide Frisbee-Catching Contest."

- At a social event with music one might say, "When I hear Latin music, I want to dance so I'm taking Salsa lessons."

It isn't absolutely essential to talk in detail about yourself and what you do. If you prefer, you can say your name and state how you happen to be at the event or in the situation. We'll expand on this shortly.

INTRODUCTION REQUIREMENTS

Whatever you choose to say initially in your introduction should be

- Shorter than 20 seconds
- Scripted ahead of time, and
- Adapted to the situation.

Assignment

Think of three Small-Talk situations in which you would likely find yourself. For each, create a:

- COMMENT based on each of the following: Event, Environment, Other Person, Yourself (that's one Comment per category for each situation). *(Note below)*

- QUESTION based on each of the following: Event, Environment, Other Person (that's one Question per category for each situation). *(Note below)*

- COMMENT FOLLOWED BY A QUESTION based on each of the following: Event, Environment, Other Person, Yourself (that's one Comment plus Question per category for each situation). *(Note below)*

- FOUR 30-SECOND INTRODUCTIONS (descriptive expansion of 20-second version).
- ✓ Topic categories and an example of each *(Note below)*

- ✓ Your introduction *(Note below)*

Read and practice these often until they become a habit and leap to mind immediately. Be sure to refine them as necessary to fit

- Your personality
- Other person
- Situation.

* * *

Reminder. Be sure to keep recording all your assignments in your *Speak Without Fear Daily Journal.*

Don't forget: **90** per cent of your success will be from *practice ... practice ... practice* plus a huge helping of *patience* and *persistence.*

This means that you *really* need to *practice ... everywhere ... all the time!*

Between events you can strike up conversations as you

- Walk the aisles of the grocery store
- Stand in line at the bank
- Talk with the teller
- Exercise at the gym
- Take your child or dog for a walk
- Get coffee on your way to work
- Get gas
- In your office at the water cooler.

It can be super-simple to practice and get used to making small talk with strangers.

For example, you and another person have stopped in front of a particular display. The other person has a product in hand. You can say, "I've never tried that before. What do you think of it?" The person responds, "I like it but it's getting very expensive." You can say, "Thanks, maybe I'll give it a try." Then you both continue on your respective ways.

As you approach the bank teller, you notice she is wearing a flattering color. You comment, "That is a very attractive color on you." She smiles and responds, "Thanks. It's a color my mother loved. She's no longer with us and I wear the outfit to remember her." You finish your business, smile, and wish her a good day.

In the gym it seems a little warmer than usual. You comment to someone passing, "Boy, it's warm in here. I hope they turn up the air-conditioning." The other person nods, "Yesterday it was freezing. They can't seem to get it right." You smile and go back to your workout.

In each scenario you've created a brief, neutral interaction with another person. Not only have you had a great practice, but you both also come away feeling touched, warmer, and more connected.

Module 9

After Introductions, Then What?

The Small-Talk Icebreakers and Introductions we have just covered are necessary for breaking into small talk. As a result, you need to work on them *daily*, using them *at every opportunity*. The more frequently you use your scripts, the more rapidly you will cement this new habit in place. And the more frequently you do it, the more confident you will be about being ready at a moment's notice to initiate a conversation and introduce yourself.

In Module 9 we are going to examine what you can do next once you have initiated the conversation and introduced yourself. Small talk is a treasure hunt wherein you are seeking little multi-faceted gems that sparkle and reflect areas of common interest.

SMALL TALK IS LIKE A GAME

Small talk is like a casual game of tennis. The goal is to keep the conversational ball in the air and make sure you both have an equal opportunity to hit the ball. For best results you need to strive for a comfortable rhythm.

Playing to your partner's strengths is more important than concentrating on demonstrating your own. Making fancy shots or acing out the other person will likely bring the conversational game to a speedy conclusion. The objective of the game should be everyone's satisfaction, a good workout, and the mutual desire for another game.

Your small-talk role models know how to play the game. They

- Listen attentively to show they are interested in the other person
- Listen attentively to fully understand what the other person is trying to communicate
- Listen so they can respond appropriately
- Listen for facts and emotion
- Are not busy thinking about what they want to say next
- Make sure they do not hog the conversation.

Instead, they work to balance the conversational input. Good conversationalists try to make small talk an equal opportunity exercise that benefits both participants. *It's the Process!*

When you work on small-talk skills, it is essential that you focus on the *process*, not the outcome. You are developing skills in both approaching and speaking with others. You are creating a format for the conversation itself ... and, then, you are systematically following it.

Whenever you are going to meet others, you need to have a short list of icebreakers—your boilerplate small-talk examples— that you can tailor to the situation and person. You should have a variety of questions, comments, etc. representing the different basic topic areas (Event, Environment, Other Person, Yourself) that we've covered.

You will also need to be practiced in using the different forms of response that we'll be covering shortly. In this way you can confidently and comfortably participate in small talk at almost any time, in any place, whenever you want.

ACTIVE LISTENING SKILLS

Active Listening is a structured way in which to give individual attention to a speaker. It is done with a genuine effort to understand the speaker's point of view and improve mutual understanding. Specifically, it is listening for meaning then checking with the speaker to see if what you think you heard was received and understood correctly. That is, is what you received congruent with the intended transmission?

To be open to understanding the other person you need to step back from your own frame of reference and suspend your judgment. This is because preconceived notions and assumptions about the other person only muddy the communication waters. As a result, hearing their message accurately becomes difficult.

Checking that the reception equals the transmission reduces the likelihood of conflict. Specifically, where there is an authentic attempt to understand and accept the other person's perspective, there is greater likelihood of cooperation, consensus, and collaboration.

WHY ACTIVE LISTENING IS NECESSARY

Too often when we interact with others, we are not fully attentive. We may be distracted, thinking about other things, such as what we want to say ... or do ...

next. When you are not tuned into the same channel as the speaker, you can make erroneous assumptions. You can misinterpret and misunderstand. Furthermore, the speaker can consciously or unconsciously sense your disengagement in the conversation. This creates discomfort in the speaker and reduces your opportunity to establish rapport and a trusting relationship with them.

OVERALL APPROACH TO ACTIVE LISTENING

For listening and responding to be effective, you need to:

- Listen with interest
- Absorb the content
- Actively grasp the facts *and* feelings you hear
- Listen for total meaning (word content plus emotion)
- Note all subtle cues
- Intuit what the person is really saying
- Sense underlying meaning
- Respond with behaviors and expressions of attention to indicate you are hearing and understanding
- Make no unfounded assumptions about the person's intentions, motivations, or expectations
- Make no unfounded assumptions about what the person means
- When verbal and nonverbal behaviors conflict, go with the nonverbal

- When you listen effectively and respond effectively, you communicate:

✓ I hear what you're feeling.
✓ I understand how you see things
✓ I see you as you are right now
✓ I am interested and/or concerned
✓ I understand where you are now (in their context)
✓ I do not judge or evaluate you as a person
✓ You do not have to be afraid of my censure for speaking out.

PRIMARY ACTIVE LISTENING TECHNIQUES

Verbal Encouragers include "Yes," "Ah," "Uh-huh," "I see," "Hmm," "Tell me more."

Nonverbal Encouragers include nodding, smiling, using voice inflection and intonation and other body language, such as subtly mirroring the speaker's behaviors.

Encouraging is straightforward. You tend to do it already. You need to be aware that you are doing both verbal and nonverbal Encouragers. They let the speaker know you're listening.

Reflecting is feeding back to the speaker the possible *emotional meaning* of what is being communicated. However, it is not simply repeating verbatim what was said.

If the speaker says, "I don't want to go to work today because I have to give a presentation," a reflective response would be, "It sounds as though you're feeling really anxious about the presentation and would prefer to avoid it." Using "It sounds as though," you are responding tentatively to what you think you have heard. You can't know for certain so you give the speaker the opportunity to confirm, deny, or reject your hypothesis.

Purposes: It helps you to

- ✓ Let the other person know you're listening
- ✓ Understand what the other is saying,
- ✓ Build rapport and trust.

Here are a few examples of *Reflecting*

- ✓ SPEAKER: "I don't think my partner is going to like

this."

- ✓ YOU: "It sounds as though you're concerned your partner will be upset."

- ✓ SPEAKER: "I hate this case. Even when I do my best, it's not appreciated."
- ✓ YOU: "It sounds as though you're concerned about others not valuing your work in it."

Assignment

- Write on a 3X5 card the word "Reflect." Then list its three Purposes: 1. Let the other person know you're listening; 2. Understand what the other is saying; 3. Build rapport and trust. And provide an example of it.

- Carry the card with you everywhere and look at it often.

- Every time you have the opportunity to try it do so. Do it first with friends and family members initially before going outside your immediate comfort zone. Then do it with strangers and others. *(Note below)*

- Get a feeling for how to do it. How have your feelings changed from doing it from the first to the last? *(Note below)*

- Notice how people respond initially and as you get better at *Reflecting* with them? *(Note below)*

- Practice, practice, practice until you feel comfortable doing this in situations where it is important to be sure that you understand correctly what the person is saying and meaning.

Once you have mastered Reflecting, go on to *Clarifying*.

Clarifying is taking Reflecting one step further. Clarifying focuses on the key underlying issues and sorting out what is confusing or conflictful. For example

✓ SPEAKER: "I really don't understand this paragraph."

   ✓ YOU: "It sounds as though it would be helpful to you to go over it again."

   ✓ SPEAKER: "I want this situation resolved as soon as possible."

   ✓ YOU: "It sounds as though timing is particularly important in this matter."

This also is tentative since you do not know for sure. You are giving the speaker the opportunity to confirm, deny, reject, or clarify your hypothesis.

Other responses that prompt *Clarifying* include:

✓ "Tell me more about that"

✓ "I'm not sure I understand what you're saying"

✓ "Would you ask/state that differently?"

Assignment

- Write on a 3X5 card the word "Clarify." Then list its Purposes: 1. Let the other person know you're listening; 2. Understand what the other is saying; 3. Build rapport and trust. And provide an example of it.

- Carry the card with you everywhere and look at it often.
- Every time you have the opportunity to try it do so. Do it first with friends and family members initially before going outside your immediate comfort zone. Then do it with strangers and others. *(Note below)*

- Get a feeling for how to do it. How have your feelings changed from doing it from the first to the last? *(Note below)*

- Notice how people respond initially and as you get better at *Clarifying* with them? *(Note below)*

- Practice, practice, practice until you feel comfortable doing this in situations where it is important to be sure that you understand correctly what the person is saying and meaning.

- Once you have mastered Clarifying, go on to Interpreting.

Interpreting is offering possible explanations for certain behaviors—as an hypothesis, *not* as a fact. These likewise are tentative. If accurate and well-timed, it can be very useful. For example, you might say, "I've noticed that when you say you want to redo your will, you shake your head. Could this indicate that you really don't want to or have qualms about it?"

This observation gives the other person a chance to consider the validity of your hunch and confirm, deny, reject, or clarify.

Other responses that enhance Interpretation include:

✓ "If I understand you correctly, you are asking/stating ___"
✓ "You seem to have a ___."

Assignment

- Write on a 3X5 card the word "Interpreting." Then list its Purposes: 1. Let the other person know you're listening; 2. Understand what the other is saying; 3. Build rapport and trust. And provide an example of it.

- Carry the card with you everywhere and look at it often.

- Every time you have the opportunity to try it do so with friends and family members initially before going outside your immediate comfort zone. *(Note below)*

- Get a feeling for how to do it. How have your feelings changed from doing it from the first to the last? *(Note below)*

- Notice how people respond initially and as you get better at *Interpreting* with them? *(Note below)*

- Practice, practice, practice until you feel comfortable doing this in situations where it is important to be sure that you understand correctly what the person is saying and meaning.

- Once you have mastered Interpreting, go on to Questioning.

Questioning is asking for further information to enhance your understanding of what the person is conveying. It's getting you and others in touch with the underlying meaning and feelings. To do this you need to ask "what" and "how" questions. They are *open-ended* and can be responded to in many ways and, thus, are more informative than closed questions that produce "yes" or "no" answers.

For example, asking, "How do you feel when you the doctor doesn't respond to your question?" produces more, different, and richer information than asking, "Do you feel bad when you don't get any response?"

Also, consider that asking "why" questions tends to put people on the spot because these questions imply there is one right "because"-answer that they should know.

As a general rule, it is better to avoid or use sparingly "why" questions, using "what," "how," and "to what degree" questions instead.

Other responses that get to the underlying meaning or feelings include:

✓ "What do you mean by that?"
✓ "How do you feel about that? "

✓ "What are your thoughts on that?"

✓ "To what degree do you think/feel that?"

Here are a few examples of *Questioning*:

✓ SPEAKER: "I really don't understand this paragraph."

✓ YOU: "What is there about the paragraph that you don't understand?"

✓ SPEAKER: "I don't think my spouse is going to like this."

✓ YOU: "How do you think your spouse will respond?"

✓ SPEAKER: "I want this situation resolved as soon as possible."

✓ YOU: "To what degree is timing a primary concern?"

• Practice, practice, practice until you are comfortable with each of them.

Assignment

- Write on a 3X5 card the word "Questioning." Then list its Purposes: 1. Let the other person know you're listening; 2. Understand what the other is saying; 3. Build rapport and trust. And provide an example of it.

- Carry the card with you everywhere and look at it often.
- Every time you have the opportunity to try it do so with friends and family members initially before going outside your immediate comfort zone. *(Note below)*

- Get a feeling for how to do it. How have your feelings changed from doing it from the first to the last? *(Note below)*

- Notice how people respond initially and as you get better at Questioning them? *(Note below)*

- Practice, practice, practice until you feel comfortable doing this in situations where it is important to be sure that you understand correctly what the person is saying and meaning.

- Once you have mastered Questioning, go on to Empathizing.

Empathizing is sensing the subjective world of the other person and what they are experiencing. It is responding to the emotion that the speaker is conveying. If the speaker says, "This week's schedule is very frustrating," you might respond, "Leaving the house at 6 a.m., and not getting home until 9 p.m. must be exhausting."

Important: Too often when someone shares an emotion-related situation with you, your first reaction, especially if you are male, will tend to be to offer an analysis of the situation and a suggestion on a way to handle it. However, unless the person asks for your problem-solving skills, most often the speaker simply wants to convey and share their perception of a situation and its attendant emotion. They are looking for understanding and support, not your solution suggestions.

Other responses that demonstrate *Empathizing* include:

- ✓ "I understand what you're feeling" (if you can and really do). That is, Do NOT say, "I *know* how you feel" when it is a tragedy/disaster you have never experienced and can't really *know* or relate to.

Rather than conveying empathy, the comment may anger the person because it may sound insincere and patronizing.

✓ "I can understand how you might feel that way"
✓ "I can see where you are"
✓ "I can see how that might be the case"
✓ "I'm sure you feel that way
✓ "It must be very difficult to deal with such a situation"
✓ "I can see that you're hurting."

Here are a few examples of *Empathizing*:

✓ SPEAKER: "I really don't understand this paragraph."
✓ YOU: "It sounds as though you feel the language is a little confusing."

✓ SPEAKER: "I don't think my partner is going to like this."
✓ YOU: "It sounds as though you're feeling a little anxious your partner will respond negatively."

✓ SPEAKER: "I want this situation resolved as soon as possible."
✓ YOU: "It sounds as though you're feeling concerned about other situations that are dependent upon this one."

Note: Since *Empathizing* is responding to the speaker's direct or indirect expression of emotion, your empathic response needs to likewise possess an emotional component.

- Practice, practice, practice until you are comfortable with it.

Assignment

- Write on a 3X5 card the word "Empathizing." Then list its Purposes: 1. Let the other person know you're listening; 2. Understand what the other is saying; 3. Build rapport and trust. And provide and an example of it.

- Carry the card with you everywhere and look at it often.

- Every time you have the opportunity to try it do so with friends and family members initially before going outside your immediate comfort zone. *(Note below)*

- Get a feeling for how to do it. How have your feelings changed from doing it from the first to the last? *(Note below)*

- Notice how people respond initially and as you get better at *Empathizing* with them? *(Note below)*

- Practice, practice, practice until you feel comfortable doing this in situations where it is important to be sure that you understand correctly what the person is saying and meaning.
- Once you have mastered Empathizing, go on to Confronting.

Confronting is not fighting or using an aggressive tactic, despite how it may sound. It is important because in everything you do and in every interaction you have there is always the possibility of having to address something you don't like being said or done, for whatever reason.

In general, people do not know how to comfortably assert themselves to others to get what they want *without* creating ill-feelings and defensiveness on the part of that other person. Most people are reluctant to address an irritating or disagreeable situation until they are so angry that they explode, creating a larger mess. Or they swallow their anger, giving themselves heart palpitations or an ulcer. Then the anger sneaks out in strange ways which makes others confused or uncomfortable. *Confronting* gives people a way to address a situation *before* it gets out of control.

Perhaps a better definition of *Confronting* is "requesting a change of a person's specific behavior while showing respect for that person."

This "requesting" is done in such a way that the focus is on the *behavior and your feelings about* it and NOT on the person who does the behavior. It allows you to share your feelings but helps you avoid evaluating, judging, and labeling the person for doing the behavior. When you evaluate, judge, or label the other person, he or she tends to become insulted, angry, and defensive ... and communication shuts down.

For example, instead of attacking by saying, "There *you* go again, purposely showing how bored *you* are with this," you would say, "When you look at your watch, drum your fingers, and look around the room, it makes me angry because I feel I am not being listened to or treated respectfully."

When you *Confront*, you need to

- Present data upon which your inferences are based before stating your inference
- Be clear, specific, and concrete
- Present tentatively information that is not fact; present it as an inference

When you Confront, you need to

- Use *I-Messages* throughout the confrontation, being careful, caring, and positively constructive
- ✓ This is how *I* see the situation (objective

statement of facts)

✓ This is how *I* feel (when you do ___, I feel ___)

✓ This is what *I* would like to see done as a result (I want you to ___).

When you *Confront*, you need to

• Avoid *You-Messages* which suggest accusation, criticism, and attack.

When you need to disagree, preface the disagreement with an Empathizing phrase because it shows you are listening and considering what the person is saying:

✓ "I'm sure you feel that way, *but* ... "

✓ "I can understand how you might feel that way, *but* ..."

✓ "You may be right, *but* ..."

Let me give you a couple of *Confronting* situations I have experienced:

A coaching client had been doing four sessions a month then suddenly hit a financial snag that left him "decisionally" immobilized. His progress had been phenomenal to that point, but now he had to decide whether to spend the money to achieve his personal goals which, in turn, fired his business achievements, or hang back. After the snag occurred, he cancelled his appointment (well in advance so he wasn't going to be charged for it), made another, and cancelled that as well. I confronted him in the following way:

"J., you have been making wonderful progress, much faster than most of my clients. I understand your financial concerns but also know that you know the sooner you can get these skills and confidence under your belt, the sooner your financial situation will change for the better. When weeks lapse between appointments, it is harder for you to maintain your motivation and progress.

"I am not comfortable with this situation. As a result, I see two options available to you. One is to wait to start again when you feel financially and emotionally secure about it. I do not recommend this one because most people find it easier not to start again. The other option is to have an appointment every other week, and pay at the individual appointment rate, which will keep you going until you feel ready to resume your weekly appointments."

Another was with a prospect who kept pressing me to have coaching session with her twice a week:

"L., I appreciate your eagerness to get going on your self-presentation and personal promotion but I do not do more than one session per week with clients. This is because of all the tasks on which you have to work during the week in preparation for your next appointment. I've found that clients need a week in order to truly absorb the materials I give them, figure out how they are going to do the exercises, tailor them to their personal style, then practice, practice, practice. If you would be willing to do weekly sessions, we can work together. However, if you want to have sessions more often, I'm not the coach for you."

As you can see, there is no "attacking" in Active Listening *Confronting*. It's simply a matter of saying:

- What the situation is

- How you see it
- How you feel about it
- What you'd like done.
- You express yourself but you do it respectfully.

Assignment

- Write on a 3X5 card the word "Empathizing." Then list its Purposes: 1. Let the other person know you're listening; 2. Understand what the other is saying; 3. Build rapport and trust. And provide and an example of it.

- Carry the card with you everywhere and look at it often.
- Every time you have the opportunity to try it do so with friends and family members initially before going outside your immediate comfort zone. *(Note below)*

- Get a feeling for how to do it. How have your feelings changed from doing it from the first to the last? *(Note below)*

- Notice how people respond initially and as you get better at *Confronting* them? *(Note below)*

- Practice, practice, practice until you feel comfortable doing this in situations where it is important to be sure that you understand correctly what the person is saying and meaning.

- Once you have mastered Confronting, go on to Summarizing.

Summarizing is crystallizing the statements into a cohesive whole with which you agree or disagree. For example, "It appears that you want to continue with your small-talk coaching but have some personal concerns about going out and applying them in the real world."

Assignment

- Write on a 3X5 card the word "Summarizing." Then list its Purposes: 1. Let the other person know you're listening; 2. Understand what the other is saying; 3. Build rapport and trust. And provide an example of it.

- Carry the card with you everywhere and look at it often.

- Every time you have the opportunity to try it do so with friends and family members initially before going outside your immediate comfort zone. *(Note below)*

- Get a feeling for how to do it. How have your feelings changed from doing it from the first to the last? *(Note below)*

- Notice how people respond initially and as you get better at *Summarizing* with them? *(Note below)*

- Practice, practice, practice until you feel comfortable doing this in situations where it is important to be sure that you understand correctly what the person is saying and meaning.

APPLICATION OF ACTIVE LISTENING TECHNIQUES

Dr. Signe: "David, I understand you would like to discuss a speech you're to give, is that correct?"

David: "I don't even know why I'm here today."

Dr. Signe: "That sounds as though there's something bothering you about your speech and, perhaps, you're conflicted about how to deal with it."

David: "Well, yeah, I guess so."

Dr. Signe: "Tell me more about what you want to do and we'll see how I can help."

David: "It's that damned speech for my company at our Chamber of Commerce. My boss is hopping mad that he wasn't the one chosen to do it."

Dr. Signe: "If I understand correctly, you want me to help you give a speech that your boss is against your giving?"

David: "No, no, you've got it all wrong. I knew I shouldn't have come in the first place."

Dr. Signe: "I can understand how you might feel that way at this point so let's determine what your situation is exactly and what your options are for addressing it."

David: "How do I know I can trust you to do the right thing?"

Dr. Signe: "When you suggest that I may be untrustworthy, I feel bad because the bond of trust I have with my clients is very important to me. But perhaps trust isn't the real issue. You can trust me to help *you* discover options for ways *you* can deal with your situation but *I* won't tell you what to do. If after we have talked further about your problem and you're still uncomfortable with the 'trust issue', I can give you the names of other consultants with whom you might be more comfortable."

David: "No, no, wait! I don't really mean that. I'm really bummed out by this situation. I don't want to go elsewhere."

Dr. Signe: "I can understand how anxiety and

frustration of what sounds like a big conflict-filled situation might make you edgy. Why don't you give me the big picture of your problem and we can see where we can go from there."

TO RECAP

Active Listening Skills provide you with the best ways to listen, respond, and enhance the overall communication process, to establish rapport, relationships, and trust.

Active Listening is a non-judgmental, structured way in which to understand the speaker's point of view and improve mutual understanding. It is listening for meaning then checking with the speaker to see if your reception matches their intended transmission. Active Listening reduces the likelihood of misinterpretation and misunderstanding and creates the opportunity for establishing rapport and a trusting relationship, cooperation, consensus, and collaboration ... and doing it so much more quickly.

HOW TO DETERMINE HOW TO RESPOND

Your best responses will depend upon the situation—specifically upon:

- What is said
- Context in which it is said
- What the intention seems to be
- To what degree the nonverbal behaviors match the spoken words
- How important the speaker's response is to the

situation

- How useful is it to reflect, clarify, interpret, question, confront, empathize, or summarize what is being said
- How you can benefit most by responding
- Where no special benefit presents itself, you can acknowledge the person by

✓ Smiling

✓ Nodding

✓ Saying, "Ah," "Yes," Hmm," "Uh-huh," "I see."

✓ Letting the other person know you're listening

✓ Showing understanding of what the other is saying without necessary agreement.

SMALL-TALK STRATEGIES

There are many ways to participate in a conversation—once you've initiated it—that *don't* require extensive knowledge about a subject area. The following examples are all on the topic of Starbucks.

Other person says, "I notice that Starbucks is opening another shop downtown." In response you can:

- *Ask a question* (open-ended whenever possible) - Use "what," "how," and "to what degree":

✓ "What did the new Starbucks store do to announce its opening?"

✓ "How helpful has their media coverage been?"

✓ "To what degree do you think their grand opening half-price sale has been useful?"

- *Dovetail* - Expand on or add something related to the other person's comment, statement, or question.
- ✓ You could say, "I understand that business is so good here that several more are planned for the area."

- *Ask a follow-up question*

Other person says, "I heard that there will be one company licensing three shops."

- ✓ You could ask," Licensing? So, Starbuck isn't a franchise?"

- *Make a general comment*
- ✓ "Investing in Starbucks would have been a moneymaker."

- *Make a specific comment*

   "I tend not to invest in stores."

- ✓ *End a comment with a question*
- ✓ "If I could go back in time, I would buy Starbucks stock at pennies a share. What would you do?"

- *Refer to previous conversations*
- ✓ "Last time you were here, you mentioned you had at one time thought of opening a coffee shop."

- *Personalize the topic*
- ✓ "If I had a real coffee shop, I'd personally want to try all the different kinds of coffee beans."

- *Clarify what was said*

Focus on the key underlying issues and sorting out confusing, conflicting issues or feelings.

- ✓ When a speaker says, "I'd hate having a Starbucks store at the mall,"
- ✓ You could clarify by saying, "It sounds as though you'd like to have a store but not in that location."
- ✓ The speaker could then confirm, deny or further explain what they meant.

- *Interpret what was said*
- ✓ Offer possible explanations for certain behaviors as an hypothesis, not as a fact.
- ✓ You might say, "I noticed that when you said you'd like to license a Starbucks, you shook your head. Could there be something about that arrangement you wouldn't like?"
- ✓ This observation gives the other person a chance to consider the validity of your hunch and confirm, deny, or clarify anyway."

Assignment

- Create a series of index cards with each card containing four Small-Talk Strategies. That's five cards—the last card has only two strategies on it.

- For one week practice daily the four strategies on card #1 every chance you get. Over the 7 days you will likely be able to try each of the four several times. What strategies did you practice? What happened? *(Note below)*

- Then for the next week go to card #2 and do the same thing for 7 days. What strategies did you practice? What happened? *(Note below)*

- Continue until you have gone through all the index cards.

You want to become familiar and comfortable with each strategy so you can call them up easily and quickly when they are appropriate. In this way you will always be ready for any conversation. As you go through the strategies, you will find ones you prefer, ones that become habits more readily. However, you will want to have the others in reserve for times when you need them specifically. Your objective is to be prepared so you're never left trying to think of something, anything, to say on the spur of the moment. When you don't know what to expect, you are more likely to feel anxious and struggle with a response.

THINGS TO REMEMBER ABOUT CONVERSATIONS

Your opening conversational gambit needs to be not only situation-specific and non-threatening but also *without assumptions*. We carry around a garbage bag full of assumptions about strangers and other people interacting with us that we project onto each new conversation ... and should not.

- Who they are
- What they are
- What they do
- What attitudes they hold
- How they think
- What they like
- Their financial status
- Their occupation
- Their marital status
- If we approve or not

BUT MOSTLY ... and this is the potentially "dangerous" part:

- They will understand what you think, feel, and want

- They will understand your motivations and intentions
- They will know what you mean by your specific questions, comments, and disclosure.

NO MIND READING

Consider that if people who really know you well can have great difficulty figuring out what you are thinking, believing, assuming, or feeling at any given moment, how can a stranger possibly be expected to do it. This suggests that as much as you'd like others to be able to read your mind on these occasions—to know precisely what you mean and why, they can't. They're not psychic.

Furthermore, if others can't read your mind, you can't read theirs either. The only way to have even an inkling of what they mean and intend is for you to pay attention to both *what they say* and *how they say it*. Then you have to look for a match among all their verbal and nonverbal behaviors. You need to ask: *Do their behaviors support the apparent meaning of their words?*

As a general rule, when you're in doubt, you should do the following:

- Rely upon the other person's nonverbal behaviors
- Feed back to them in your own words what you think they said and meant
- Ask them for confirmation or correction.

Remember: What you're striving for in conversations is to find some common ground so you have some basis for continuing the interpersonal interaction. This requires that you be sure that what you think is being said is what is being intended to be communicated. When you are comfortable you are on the right track, it is easier to look for and find areas of interest, knowledge, or experience to which the other person can relate.

TOPICS TO AVOID

It's always safer to start with neutral topics. Those that do not qualify as neutral are:

- Politics
- Religion
- Sex, sexual history, and sexual practices
- Your struggle with anxiety or small talk.

In general, they should be avoided. This is unless, of course, you're in a context that supports those topics—such as, a political rally, religious gathering, counseling session, or anxiety support group.

It's important to remember that partners in established relationships may differ in philosophy, attitudes, or views on controversial topics and still have a viable relationship. However, partners in potential relationships don't yet have a solid foundation of other acceptable factors upon which to rely. This means that newbies who differ in philosophy, attitudes, or views on *controversial* topics will tend not to continue their tentative interactions to form viable relationships.

When you are looking specifically for similarities on which to build a viable relationship and encounter, instead, dissimilarities, you are more likely to reject the other person, and/or be rejected by them.

NO INTERROGATION, PLEASE

As we've discussed, you find common ground by drawing others out with casual questions. However, you need to make sure those really are *casual* questions. You don't want to fall into the trap of asking too many questions or too personal questions. Furthermore, you especially don't want to do this in rapid-fire succession. This takes on the flavor of a police grilling.

Instead, as you listen for and offer information, you need to determine what you want to pursue. Once you have a sense of what that is, you maintain the conversation by carefully attending to and remembering the relevant information offered.

Of course, conversations don't require that the partners hold precisely the same views or agree on everything. But commonality in *some* area definitely helps. If it feels as though there are too many dissimilarities between your views, interests, philosophies, values, and goals and theirs, you may decide that the conversation is not worth your time and effort.

However, as you're getting your small-talk skills back into shape, don't be too quick to discount and dismiss such conversations. You can use these conversations as practice ... with little or no investment. It's important to note that *not* every conversation needs to be aimed at creating friendships ... or more. Use every opportunity to practice. You'll become better at making small talk and you might just strike up friendships along the way.

TWO BIG NO-NO'S

- Don't try to change the other person's mind
- Don't tell the other person what to do.

Those behaviors are perceived as controlling and are not conducive to further exploration of common interests or a relationship.

TWO BIG YES-YES'S

- Hold up your end of the conversation
- Take on the role of one who is socially adept.

BUT ... SOMETIMES IT DOESN'T WORK

No matter how carefully you listen, share information, and hold up your end, it is a fact that not every interaction will be successful. The Law of Averages would predict that you'd be successful only 50% of the time. Therefore, it's essential that you view this in its proper perspective.

Sometimes things just don't work out no matter how hard you try, or how assertive, polished, positive, prepared, or clever you are. You have little control over the circumstances in which you find yourself and no control over the other person. Thus, it is imperative that you recognize and accept that not all your attempts at small talk will work out. This has nothing to do with personal failure on your part.

However, if nearly every single small talk attempt results in no interaction or a negative interaction, you may want to go back and re-assess your thinking, nonverbal behavior, and small-talk strategies to make sure everything is in sync.

SMALL-TALK EXPECTATIONS

You need to keep in mind what small-talk "success" realistically means. Small-talk success is engaging another person in conversation. It's not about creating a lifelong friend or setting up a date. The success is in introducing yourself and pleasantly exchanging information with strangers and other people. It's feeling good about making a face-to-face verbal connection with another person.

If, however, the other situations develop later as a result of building on the foundation of your initial small talk ... that's great! But *don't* ... *don't* ... *don't* make finding a lifelong friend or setting up a date THE focus of your embryonic small-talk endeavors.

That focus is riddled with the pressure and tension of social anxiety that will leave you feeling unsure, vulnerable, and less confident that you can succeed at making small talk. Also, trying for a date right out of the bag is more often than not doomed to failure ... disappointment ... and a sense of rejection, especially when you're just becoming socially effective.

The *rule of thumb* for everyone, not just those with fear of small talk, is to

- Go for the simple interaction *first*
- Go for an interest-based friendship *second*
- And when you're feeling more confident in your skills, self-presentation, and the degree of similarities between you, then GO for a more intimate relationship *third*.

Module 10

Focus, Style, and Small Talk Mastery

Being successful at small talk isn't rocket science. In fact, it's really quite simple. Once you get the fundamental automatic negative thoughts and anxious feelings under control. And once you get the basic small talk strategies under your belt, being a successful conversationalist is purely a matter of mindset.

HOW TO BE A SUCCESSFUL CONVERSATIONALIST

Being a conversationalist is primarily an attitudinal focus. It's the thing that separates those who make a good impression from those who don't.

Part of that focus is to bring out the best in the other person. If you listen carefully to what the other person is saying, you can identify commonalities and bonds then use this as a springboard for your questions and comments.

By acknowledging that the other has something important to say—something to which you want to listen—you make the other conversation participant feel good about her/himself *and* about you. The person is more likely to see you as similar and feel attracted to you. They will sense your sincerity and this will foster their liking and trusting you.

The second part of that focus is to bring out the best in you. To be an interesting and enjoyable conversationalist, even in small talk, you have to truly believe you are. If you think that what you say is stupid or of no consequence or that you don't even want to try, the other person will pick up on your slightest negative nonverbal behavior and mirror it.

As a result, they will tend to see you as standoffish, arrogant, negative, or detached and feel no value in talking with you. But if you believe you have something worthwhile to share, that you want to share, others will be attracted to you and be open to your sharing. Your focus creates the image you project.

WHAT IS YOUR CONVERSATIONAL STYLE?

Everyone has a conversational style or preference. What's yours? Your evolving small-talk skills will work hand in hand with your *conversational style*. It's what you do in small talk and how you do it.

To find out yours ask yourself:

- Do you tend to tell stories or relate personal experiences?
- Do you tend to be analytical and break things down into their components?
- Do you probe for what others are thinking, getting them to talk?
- Do you deal with facts, logic, sequences, and concepts?
- Do you look for feelings, opinions, and relationships?

- Do you interpret happenings and place them in the bigger picture?
- Do you creatively flit from subject to subject?
- Do you talk about anything to keep the conversation going?

What this tells you—something that's easy to forget—is that other people don't necessarily talk about things the same way you do. This means you may be talking about facts and the other person is talking about feelings. You may be relating an anecdote and the other person is already on to another topic.

Consequently, there can be a mismatch. Mismatches can cause you to experience that nagging sense that something isn't right or isn't working. But a mismatch doesn't have to stop the conversation.

If you are aware of your style and can determine the style of the other person, you can make a conscious decision to accept the difference *if* the small-talk potential seems worth it. You can make minor adjustments to your expectations for these circumstances. On the other hand, if it doesn't seem worth your effort, you can decide that you don't want to continue and let it go or just use it for practice.

However, as I've mentioned before, continuing the conversation is *good* practice and hones your skills further. I still do this even if the conversation isn't particularly important to me or going anywhere in particular. I also do it to create a positive impression when it's important to me.

It's important to remember that one style is not better than another. They're just different, like people.

Assignment

- What is your style? Can you name it? *(Note below)*

- Describe how you prefer to converse. *(Note below)*

- Look at people you know. What is their style? *(Note below)*

- Look at celebrities you like. What is their style? *(Note below)*

- Record your observations in your *Speak Without Fear Daily Journal.*

STEP BACK A MINUTE TO LOOK AT YOUR PROGRESS

When you encounter a stranger or group of strangers now, you are no longer like a steward on the Titanic in turbulent seas as it hits an iceberg. You are now like the captain of a rowboat on a calm lake. You are moving your sturdy small-talk craft forward with confidence, competence, and effectiveness.

What keeps your small talk vessel moving with confidence, competence, and effectiveness is your using O-A-Rs. O-A-R is the behavioral principles on which every face-to-face conversation is based. It is the umbrella under which all the small-talk strategies you have learned, and will learn, are catalogued. Specifically, O-A-R refers to:

- Observing others
- Asking questions
- Revealing something about yourself.

Keeping O-A-Rs in mind, we will move from the specific small- talk strategies to address more general situations and how you can practically and confidently approach them.

HOW AND WHERE TO START THE SMALL-TALK SEQUENCE

At any gathering—whether social or business, informal or formal—it is important for you to meet as many people as possible. Doing so allows you to continue to practice and sharpen your interaction skills. It also makes each individual encounter less important and less anxiety provoking.

Why? As the process becomes more casual for you, the amount of pressure on you diminishes. Furthermore, the amount of risk associated with each interaction drops significantly.

One excellent way to meet lots of people is to station yourself near the entrance to the event. As people arrive, you can make eye contact with them, smile, and welcome them. You act as a greeter. You do this as if you were part of the sponsoring organization. Specifically, you act like a *host*, not a guest. (More about this shortly.)

As you greet them, you should first say your name. Then you should look at their nametag and repeat their name after they say it.

This does three things for you.

- First, it gets your name before them.
- Second, it helps you remember their name.
- Third, it lets the other person not only hear their name (which always feels good) but also hear if you've said it correctly. If not, it gives them the chance to correct it.

WHY ACTING LIKE A HOST IS IMPORTANT?

It will immediately get you in contact with those who are attending.

- It allows you to determine the people with whom you want to speak later.
- It makes your speaking with them later easier because you will already have broken the ice with them.
- It is through your initial brief interaction you will create a friendly and positive impression for later.

- It will enable you to later locate those people of interest more easily.

- When you see any of them later, they will recognize you and feel positive about you.

If positioning yourself by the entrance is either not feasible or too anxiety provoking, you can volunteer to be at the reception table where nametags are given out. While this will make your interaction with others briefer than if you were greeting them at the door, it still allows you to meet people in a protected, one-on-one environment.

A third possibility is for you to station yourself by the buffet table or bar. This, however, has the difficulty of trying to talk with others whose attention is divided. If they are jockeying with others to get food or a drink, you may not have their full attention. Still, it can be useful for either an initial interaction or a subsequent one.

Be sure to introduce yourself to the hosts or leaders of the function. If it's a social occasion, thank them for having the function. If it's business, indicate your interest or enthusiasm in being there and being a part of it. Of course, exactly what you say will depend upon the specific circumstances of the event.

Note: It is perfectly all right to tell someone that they look familiar if they do. In general, it is better to act on that than not to act on it. This is because the person may be someone you have met who is wondering why you are not acknowledging them. This can create confusion and a negative impression.

However, when you speak to the person, do NOT say, "Do you remember me?" This makes people defensive and uncomfortable because it puts them on the spot. Acting as a *host*, you want to make sure your guests are comfortable.

Instead, say that the person looks familiar but at the moment you can't recall their name or where you may have met them. People generally are very gracious about this and will fill in the blanks for you or tell you that they don't know you. And even if it turns out you don't know the person, you have already broken the ice and can strike up a conversation.

YOU APPROACH THEM

As you saw with your acting like a host, it's advisable, whenever possible, for you to take the *active* approach. That is, *you* are the one to introduce yourself to the other person. Being the conversation initiator has numerous advantages over being approached by others.

- You have more control of the situation.
- You are choosing the person to approach.
- You are preparing what to say, how to say it, and tailoring it to the person.
- You get to make the first statement or ask the first question.
- You get to present the initial topic and direct the conversation.
- You aren't awkwardly waiting and anticipating, someone to approach you.
- You aren't wondering and worrying what they'll say and how you'll respond—waiting and anticipating engender panic.

Remember. Panic severs the connection between your brain and your tongue. This often leaves you speechless, stuttering, or babbling, your mind racing to think of something to say. None of which is conducive to creating a good first impression.

WORKING YOUR WAY UP TO IT

You can also look for people who are obviously more anxious than you are. They are the people who are on the outer periphery of the crowd. They may be sitting or standing by themselves. They are the ones with that deer in the headlights look, who are clutching their drinks or paper plates with white knuckled hands. At one time or another, you've probably been there and done that. I know I have.

Talking with them will give you practice. It shifts your focus from your needs to the other person's needs (which are obviously greater than your own). Helping out a fellow sufferer can further add to you sense of social strength and confidence.

Furthermore, if you have already made the acquaintance of someone else there, you can then introduce this new person to him or her. Once again you are acting as a host and looking confident and leader-like. Your generosity will leave a good impression on both parties.

Assignment

- Ask yourself: Exactly what does a host do? *(Note below)*

- Watch someone who is a host or acts like one and observe host-like behaviors. What are they specifically? *(Note below)*

- Rehearse emulating their behaviors in private. What behaviors did you emulate? How did it go? *(Note below)*

- Then practice acting like a host at you next social opportunity. What did you do? Where did you do it? How did others respond to you? How do you feel it went? *(Note below)*

- Start small with one or two behaviors and then add on to them. This can provide a level of comfort and control you cannot achieve in your role as a guest. What did you start with? What did you add to it? How do you feel about it? *(Note below)*

YOU DON'T HAVE TO DO IT ALONE

Another technique that many find helpful is having a buddy with you when you walk in the door. It is particularly useful if this is a person who is more comfortable with small talk than you are. Having this person handy can give you a sense of support and confidence.

You two can introduce each other around, both of you acting like hosts. However, it is important that you NOT stay together. You both need to circulate. It does not help you to feel dependent on this other person for company and courage.

However, having this person there can help keep you feeling more secure, just in case you need them. Specifically, you can arrange with your partner to have a signal that you can flash to them if you need assistance. You want to have this as a fail-safe mechanism only, NOT as a lifeline.

Instead, you need to rely upon yourself and use your bag full of small-talk strategies and relaxation techniques so you don't have to ask for assistance. You can have your buddy check on you periodically from a distance and come to your rescue, but *only* when *absolutely* necessary. Ninety-nine percent of the time just knowing that person is there is enough to negate your need for a rescue.

Assignment

- Make arrangements with a friend to be a social event buddy. What did you arrange? *(Note below)*

- Take your buddy to an event to see to what degree having them there adds to your confidence and competence level. How did you feel just knowing they were there? *(Note below)*

- Compare your thoughts, feelings, and actions when having a buddy present with when you didn't have a buddy present. *(Note below)*

- Record your findings in your *Speak Without Fear Journal.*

HOW TO ENTER GROUPS

When you find a group that you would like to join, it is essential that you *first* watch their body language and listen to the tone of their conversation. Before you do anything else, you need to ask yourself:

- Do they look as if they are huddled together, keeping something private to themselves?

- Do they sound as if they are discussing something very intensely or seriously?

If *yes* to either, this group may not be open to outsiders, at least not at this moment. They may be discussing business or something very private that they do not want to share with anyone else.

When you find a group of interest that looks less intense, you *first* need to determine if there is physical space for you to join in the conversation. If there seems to be space, you then need to position yourself close to the group.

Initially you should not say anything. Instead, you can give low-key facial feedback to what is being said. That is, you smile, nod, etc., but are not overly dramatic in doing so, such that you draw attention to yourself.

When someone acknowledges you verbally *or* makes solid eye contract with you (not a quick sidelong glance) and looks positive (not annoyed or questioning), you can feel free to join the group.

If group members look to you as if to ask your name, smile and introduce yourself but leave it at that unless you're prompted to say more. Once you're in, it is better for you not to offer an opinion immediately. Opinion making is considered a perk of being a member of the group and you are not a member yet. This means you need to listen a while and continue to use your nonverbal behavior, adding "uh-huh" where appropriate.

You can wait until someone looks at you or asks you for your input or you can wait for a lull in the conversation to become involved. Adhering to group conversation etiquette further cements your acceptance into the group. Now you can feel more comfortable offering your opinions.

BUT when you actually join in the discussion, you need to stay within the group's current topic. It is not appropriate for you to introduce your own topic, not yet anyway.

What are the reasons for this?

- First, you are a "newbie." You need to get the lay of the land and determine the ground rules.

- Second, you are an invited *guest* in *their* group.

  You can become involved in the conversation by simply:

- Asking a question of clarification ("Where did you find that Starbucks information?")

- Agreeing with a statement ("I found that as well in some research I did.")

When you participate, be sure the topic about which you wish to speak is appropriate and within the realm of what they have been talking about. If there is to be a dramatic change in what the group is discussing, you, as a newbie, are not the one to create that change.

Remember: Group members tend to be possessive of their territory and authority. Courtesy in waiting to be invited into topic selection is expected and appreciated by the group.

Assignment

- Observe different groups speaking.
- Look to see how outsiders enter the group. What do they do? How does it work for them? *(Note below)*

- Practice approaching and entering with different groups to find what works best under what circumstances. What did you try? What worked best? *(Note below)*

- Record your findings in your *Speak Without Fear Journal.*

HOW TO HANDLE AWKWARD CONVERSATIONS

In general, if you are at a gathering where your goal is to mingle and meet people, you should limit your conversations with any one individual to approximately 5 minutes. If you find yourself with someone who is uninteresting, bragging, not listening to you, negative or rude, you need to excuse yourself ASAP and move on.

If the person is constantly changing the subject, you have to decide for yourself if you want to let them run the conversation. If the conversation is interesting but you're not sure how to respond to topics you know little about, you can use any number of Small-Talk Techniques, such as asking questions or having the person expand, clarify, or relate it to other things.

HOW TO HANDLE CONFLICT

Occasionally you will encounter conflict in your small-talk interactions. There are a number of ways you can address it so you stay in control. Your best responses will depend upon the situation, specifically upon:

- What is said
- What the context is
- What the intention seems to be
- To what degree their nonverbal behaviors match their spoken words
- How important the comment and the situation are for you to choose to respond
- How useful is it to question, clarify, interpret, give feedback, summarize, or confront what is being said
- How you benefit most by responding.

Where there appears to be no benefit to verbally addressing it, you can choose to

- Smile knowingly and ignore the comment
- Nod and ignore the comment
- Inquire to find out what it really means
- Indicate you heard the person, but express your agreement or disagreement and repeat that as necessary.

Whatever you choose, you need to step away emotionally from the conflict. Take on the disengaged, objective role of a television reporter. (This takes practice!) This will allow you to stay in control, to say what you want to say and do what you want to do and not be at the mercy of someone pushing your "hot buttons." This will allow you to feel good about yourself and about how you handled the situation.

WHEN YOU NEED TO CHALLENGE SOME BEHAVIOR

When you need to actually challenge some specific behavior, you need to do it so that the focus is on the behavior and your feelings about it, and not on the person who does the behavior. (This is *Confronting* in Active Listening.)

For example, "When I don't understand immediately what you mean, you roll your eyes and say, 'Never mind.' This makes me angry because I feel I'm not being treated respectfully."

This allows you to share your feelings but, at the same time, avoid judging, evaluating, or labeling the other person. Judging, evaluating or labeling the person creates defensiveness and anger. These generally will stop all communication ... cold.

BECAUSE THIS IS SO IMPORTANT IT IS BEING REITERATED:

When you confront, you need to

- Present the facts upon which your inferences are based before you state your inference
- Be clear, specific, and concrete
- Present information that is not fact as an inference
- Use *I-messages* throughout the confrontation, being careful, caring, and positively constructive

I-MESSAGES

- This is how I see the situation (objective statement of facts)
- This is how I feel about it ("When you do ___, I feel ___ ")
- This is what I would like to see done as a result ("I want you to ___.")

All these skills help you to be firm and stick to your firmness. They are the basic scripted responses you need to *memorize* because conflict and confrontation immediately trigger anxiety. As you know, anxiety erases access to your brain. When you have memorized the I-Message approach and made it a *habit*, you don't have to worry about searching your brain at a moment's notice for the right way to solve the problem. You know automatically how to respond each time you encounter conflict or feel you want to confront the other person.

Knowing what to expect and being prepared with the way to respond is foundational to creating confidence and increasing your chances of making yourself heard and getting you what you want.

Assignment

- Pick a conflict situation wherein you did not express yourself as assertively as you would have liked. What was it? *(Note below)*

- Give a summary of what happened, what the other person said and did, and what you said and did. *(Note below)*

- If this were to happen again, how could you now express yourself, using your *Confronting* guidelines, in order to stand up for yourself and respectfully state what you want? *(Note below)*

- Make sure that you use I-messages and not you-messages.

- Record this did in your *Speak Without Fear Daily Journal.*

HOW TO GRACEFULLY LEAVE A CONVERSATION

If for any reason you want to exit a conversation, you should begin by exhibiting subtle "exiting" body language. This is because most of our interactions are guided by nonverbal behaviors. These are what people pick up on first.

To begin with, you might angle your body away from the other person. If you're seated, you might put your hands on the chair arm rests. If standing and near a door, you might put your hand on the doorknob. You might look less at the speaker, shifting your focus and glancing away a little. You might give shorter responses and more "uh-huh" replies.

You might look less eager, interested, enthusiastic, or inquisitive. You might nod slightly more rapidly as if to suggest you are in a hurry for the other to finish. You might shift your weight from one foot to the other, indicating an interest in making a change.

You might smile but with your lips together and your eyes not involved. You might nod or dip your head so that you are not looking at the speaker as frequently. Furthermore, you might drop verbal cues that you are ready to leave.

Any one or combination of these will generally get the other person's attention and alert them as to the imminent change. So frequently you don't have to do much to get your message subtly across. However, sometimes people appear oblivious and it may take several nonverbal and verbal behaviors together to get their attention.

In any conversational situation, when you are finally ready to make the break, you need to respond to what the speaker was saying and immediately follow it with a big sincere smile and, "I've have really enjoyed talking with you about (whatever the topic was) but ..."

The "but ..." is where you add your reason for breaking off the conversation. You can say, "I need to keep circulating" or "I want to say 'hi' to some old friends." Whatever you say, it should be pleasant and polite, and should not sound like an elaborate excuse.

Confident people don't make elaborate excuses. They don't need to. They are in control.

If you found the person particularly interesting and would like to talk with them again, be sure to let them know. Then see if you can arrange to get in touch by exchanging e-mail addresses or phone numbers.

BUT WHAT IF THE PERSON HAS BEEN OBNOXIOUS?

What should you do when leaving if the other person has made the conversation unbearable? Sometimes people hog the floor. Sometimes they don't listen to what you have to say. Sometimes they brag, complain, whine or are just plain rude to you.

There is no need to reward unacceptable or negative behavior. But, irrespective of their behavior, you should *always* keep *your* small talk positive and respectful. That is not to say you should tell them you enjoyed the conversation if you did not. Instead, you should pleasantly excuse yourself ASAP ... and move on.

Assignment

- Watch socially effective people as they leave conversations. Whom did you watch? *(Note below)*

- Make note of how they make their exits positive and smooth. What specifically did they do and in what sequence? *(Note below)*

- Check out good low-risk places in which to practice your initiating and exiting skills, such as association meetings, community events, and— believe it or not—singles' bars. What places have you chosen? *(Note below)*

- Model their conversation-exiting behaviors in casual environments. What behaviors did you model? How did they work? *(Note below)*

- Record your observations in your *Speak Without Fear Journal.*

WHAT IF THE OTHER PERSON WANTS TO LEAVE FIRST?

If you can want to leave a conversation, this means that others can want to leave it as well. By the way, this can be for lots reasons that have little or nothing to do with you. Thus, don't feel insulted, inadequate, or like a failure. This means it is imperative that you also be able to recognize the "I gotta go" nonverbal clues in others so you can respond confidently.

The moment you start to see fidgeting or distracted behavior, you need to be the *first* one to say "good-bye." As soon as you spot it, look for an appropriate opening to let your listener know that you have found it a pleasure speaking with them about the topic, if you have. However, if they were miserable people, you should omit this part. Then you should smile and indicate you need to "keep circulating" or "say 'hi' to old friends" (or whatever).

By going first, you take control. You keep yourself from being caught in the awkward "Now, what do I say?" trap. Moreover, your conversation partner will be relieved that they do not have to dance around, trying to get your attention, anxiously hoping you'll get the message. Your being aware of signs and acting on them will be a win-win situation.

LEAVING THE EVENT

When ready to leave the event, be sure to say "good-bye" to the host or leader. Thank them and tell them you enjoyed the gathering or learned a lot, depending upon the function of the event. If you see any of the people with whom you arranged to be in contact, let them know you're leaving and that you'll be in touch as arranged.

If they are speaking with someone when you approach and no one acknowledges you right away, wait for a pause in the conversation (if possible), and say, "If I could interrupt for just one moment (to both people), I have to leave now and I will be in touch with you (to the person of interest)." Resist the impulse to say, "I'm sorry to interrupt ..." Instead of sounding polite, it tends to come across as timid and lacking in confidence.

GOING THAT EXTRA MILE ...

Remember: Sometimes you have to go that extra mile to achieve your goal and get what you want. To quote playwright George Bernard Shaw from *Mrs. Warren's Profession*:

"The people who get on in this world are the people who get up and look for the circumstances they want, and, if they can't find them, make them."

YOUR SMALL-TALK REMINDER CHECKLIST

While communication is a focus of every small-talk interaction, no two people communicate alike. Moreover, what's acceptable and expected by individuals may vary to some degree from region to region, country to country, and culture to culture. Because communication is somewhat fluid, there are no absolute rules to follow in small talk.

Therefore, what you have learned in the *How to Speak Without Fear Small Talk Course* have been principles and norms that most people understand, accept, and adhere to. These principles guide you to:

- What people tend to expect in small talk
- What generally works.

These principles provide you with flexibility so you can apply your small-talk skills to almost all situations with confidence and competence.

ALWAYS DO THE FOLLOWING:

- Think before communicating. Plan what you'll say and how you'll say it.
- Decide on the purpose of your communication. Know what is to be achieved.
- Take into consideration the situation and circumstances in which the communication is to take place.
- Make the message complete, specific, using a frame of reference. Tie it into something.
- Make verbal and nonverbal behaviors match and be consistent.
- Make the message fit with and be appropriate to the receiver.
- Listen carefully to what is said and how it's said.
- Provide feedback to the sender of the message.
- Describe behavior without making evaluations or judgments.
- Don't make assumptions or jump to conclusions.
- Respect the ideas of others.
- Acknowledge your feelings and those of others.
- Control your emotions.
- Use a win/win approach where you and others both get something you want.

YOU'VE DONE IT!

You've successfully completed the *How to Speak Without Fear Small Talk Course!*

You've worked hard and you've achieved your small talk goal! You have created small talk confidence, competence, and effectiveness. Bravo!

But, ALWAYS REMEMBER, that your small-talk skills and social effectiveness are like muscles. They need *frequent* exercise to keep them toned, healthy, and at their best. Even habits when not practiced lose their habitual function. Your participation in this learning experience does *not* end with your doing the last assignment in this course.

No, this course is only the beginning ... the first step in your conversational success future. And now ... a whole new world is opening up to you. Ahead of you are opportunities galore for fun, relationships ... and much more.

I wish you all success on your small talk journey because:

You Deserve It!

Dr. Signe
Your Social Effectiveness Coach

ABOUT THE AUTHOR

Signe A. Dayhoff, Ph.D., M.A., M.Ed., is a Social Psychologist and cognitive-behaviorist, with post-graduate training in counseling. She received her doctorate from Boston University where she studied ways to increase personal and professional presentation and self-promotion effectiveness using interpersonal communication skills. For the last 37 years she has coached internationally and taught individuals how to transform presentation anxiety and self-promotion reluctance into confident social effectiveness.

Currently she is president of Effectiveness-Plus LLC, which provides educational products and services. A Certified Graduate of Authentic Happiness Coaching (Positive Psychology), she coaches internationally and is a member of International Coach Federation and International Association of Coaches.

Prior to this, she was president of The Mentoring Network, which provided mentoring and training in interpersonal skills for career development. She has taught psychology at Boston University, University of Massachusetts, and Framingham State College and has done research at Massachusetts Institute of Technology, Fairview State Hospital, and Scripps Clinic and Research Foundation.

For four years she produced and hosted Continental Cablevision's alternative-career-development program, the *Inside Track*, in Wellesley, Massachusetts. For it she received a Conti Award nomination.

She has been quoted in publications including *Industry Week*, *Wall Street Journal*, *Success*, *Executive Travel*, *Time Out New York*, *Shape*, and *Cosmopolitan*, and has written for the *Boston Business Journal*.

She is the author of 17 books, including:

- *Create Your Own Career Opportunities*, a guide to self-promotion through creating visibility and credibility, used at Pepperdine University
- *Diagonally-Parked in a Parallel Universe: Working Through Social Anxiety* (2nd Edition), acclaimed by leading clinical researchers and therapists in the field
- *Growing Up "Unacceptable": How Katharine Hepburn Rescued Me*
- *Get the Job You Want: Successful Strategies for Selling Yourself in the Job Market*
- *How to Win in a Tough Job Market: Successful Strategies for Getting the Job You Want*
- *Promote Myself? I'd Rather Eat Works: 21 Simple Steps to Confidentially Tooting Your Own Horn to Achieve Your Career and Life Goals*
- *What No One Told You: How Insiders Really Get Jobs*
- *Scared of Your Boss? Smash Through Your Fear Now*
- *Single and Multiple Mentors: Perceived Effects on Managerial Success*
- *Decision Making for Managers* (for AMACOM's Education for Management).

- Contributed to books such as David Riklan's *101 Great Ways to Improve Your Life (Vol. 2)* and Steven J. Bennett's *Executive Chess: Creative Problem Solving by 45 of America's Top Business Leaders and Thinkers.*

She is also an applied feline behaviorist, "kitty mom" to 20-plus rescued elderly, disabled, and chronically-ill cats, and is author of cat memoirs:

- *What Faust the Dancing Cat Taught Me*
- *Faust the Dancing Cat Tackles Strippers, Scammers & Bears*
- *Faust the Dancing Cat Does Vegas*
- *Remarkable Tales of Cats Who Whisper to Humans*
- *How Intrepid the Disabled Kitten Triumphed to Help Others.*

www.ingramcontent.com/pod-product-compliance
Lightning Source LLC
Chambersburg PA
CBHW060247050426
42448CB00009B/1588